Helen Keller

GREAT ACHIEVERS

LIVES OF THE PHYSICALLY CHALLENGED

Helen Keller

HUMANITARIAN

Lois P. Nicholson

Chelsea House Publishers

New York • Philadelphia

CHELSEA HOUSE PUBLISHERS

EDITORIAL DIRECTOR   Richard Rennert
EXECUTIVE MANAGING EDITOR   Karyn Gullen Browne
COPY CHIEF   Robin James
PICTURE EDITOR   Adrian G. Allen
CREATIVE DIRECTOR   Robert Mitchell
ART DIRECTOR   Joan Ferrigno
PRODUCTION MANAGER   Sallye Scott

GREAT ACHIEVERS: LIVES OF THE PHYSICALLY CHALLENGED

SENIOR EDITOR   Kathy Kuhtz Campbell
SERIES DESIGN   Basia Niemczyc

Staff for **HELEN KELLER**
EDITORIAL ASSISTANT   Scott D. Briggs
PICTURE RESEARCHER   Sandy Jones
COVER ILLUSTRATION   Michael Garland

First Printing

1 3 5 7 9 8 6 4 2

Library of Congress Cataloging-in-Publication Data

Nicholson, Lois.
Helen Keller: humanitarian / Lois P. Nicholson.
p. cm.—(Great achievers)
Includes bibliographical references and index.
ISBN 0-7910-2086-X.
     0-7910-2099-1 (pbk.)
1. Keller, Helen, 1880–1968—Juvenile literature. 2. Blind-deaf—United States—
Biography —Juvenile literature. [1. Keller, Helen, 1880–1968. 2. Blind. 3. Deaf.
4. Physically handicapped. 5. Women—Biography.] I. Title. II. Series: Great achievers (Chelsea House Publishers)
HV1624.K4N53 1995   94-37512
362.4'1'092—dc20   CIP

FRONTISPIECE

*In November 1955, Major General Melvin Maas, who is blind and
is chairman of the Committee on Employment of the Physically
Handicapped, awards Helen Keller a citation for her humanitarian
work. Twin sisters Barbara and Jolee Crane, both of whom have been
blind since birth, present Keller with a handwoven tray that they made
as students at the New York Institute for the Blind and as Girl Scouts.*

CONTENTS

GREAT ACHIEVERS

LIVES OF THE PHYSICALLY CHALLENGED

A Message for Everyone

Jerry Lewis

Close to half a century ago—when I was the ripe old age of 23—an incredible stroke of fate rocketed me to overnight stardom as an entertainer. After the initial shock wore off, I began to have a very strong feeling that, in return for all life had given me, I must find a way of giving something back. At just that moment, a deeply moving experience in my personal life persuaded me to take up the leadership of a fledgling battle to defeat a then little-known group of diseases called muscular dystrophy, as well as other related neuromuscular diseases—all of which are disabling and, in the worst cases, cut life short.

In 1950, when the Muscular Dystrophy Association (MDA)—of which I am national chairman—was established, physical disability was looked on as a matter of shame. Franklin Roosevelt, who guided America through World War II from a wheelchair, and Harold Russell, the World War II hero who lost both hands in battle, then became an Academy Award–winning movie star and chairman of the President's Committee on Employment of the Handicapped, were the exceptions. One of the reasons that muscular dystrophy and related diseases were so little known was that people who had been disabled by them were hidden at home, away from the pity and discomfort with which they were generally regarded by society. As I got to know and began working with people who have disabilities, I quickly learned what a tragic mistake this perception was. And my determination to correct this terrible problem soon became as great as my commitment to see disabling neuromuscular diseases wiped from the face of the earth.

I have long wondered why it never occurs to us, as we experience the knee-jerk inclination to feel sorry for people who are physically disabled, that lives such as those led by President Roosevelt, Harold Russell, and all of the extraordinary people profiled in this Great Achievers series demonstrate unmistakably how wrong we are. Physical disability need not be something that blights life and destroys opportunity for personal fulfillment and accomplishment. On the contrary, as people such as Ray Charles, Stephen Hawking, and Ron Kovic prove, physical disability can be a spur to greatness rather than a condemnation of emptiness.

In fact, if my experience with physically disabled people can be taken as a guide, as far as accomplishment is concerned, they have a slight edge on the rest of us. The unusual challenges they face require finding greater-than-average sources of energy and determination to achieve much of what able-bodied people take for granted. Often, this ultimately translates into a lifetime of superior performance in whatever endeavor people with disabilities choose to pursue.

If you have watched my Labor Day Telethon over the years, you know exactly what I am talking about. Annually, we introduce to tens of millions of Americans people whose accomplishments would distinguish them regardless of their physical conditions—top-ranking executives, physicians, scientists, lawyers, musicians, and artists. The message I hope the audience receives is not that these extraordinary individuals have achieved what they have by overcoming a dreadful disadvantage that the rest of us are lucky not to have to endure. Rather, I hope our viewers reflect on the fact that these outstanding people have been ennobled and strengthened by the tremendous challenges they have faced.

In 1992, MDA, which has grown over the past four decades into one of the world's leading voluntary health agencies, established a personal achievement awards program to demonstrate to the nation that the distinctive qualities of people with disabilities are by no means confined to the famous. What could have been more appropriate or timely in that year of the implementation of the 1990 Americans with Disabilities Act than to take an action that could perhaps finally achieve the alteration of public perception of disability, which MDA had struggled over four decades to achieve?

On Labor Day, 1992, it was my privilege to introduce to America MDA's inaugural national personal achievement award winner, Steve Mikita, assistant attorney general of the state of Utah. Steve graduated magna cum laude from Duke University as its first wheelchair student in history and was subsequently named the outstanding young lawyer of the year by the Utah Bar Association. After he spoke on the Telethon with an eloquence that caused phones to light up from coast to coast, people asked me where he had been all this time and why they had not known of him before, so deeply impressed were they by him. I answered that he and thousands like him have been here all along. We just have not adequately *noticed* them.

It is my fervent hope that we can eliminate indifference once and for all and make it possible for all of our fellow citizens with disabilities to gain their rightfully high place in our society.

ON FACING CHALLENGES

John Callahan

I was paralyzed for life in 1972, at the age of 21. A friend and I were driving in a Volkswagen on a hot July night, when he smashed the car at full speed into a utility pole. He suffered only minor injuries. But my spinal cord was severed during the crash, leaving me without any feeling from my diaphragm downward. The only muscles I could move were some in my upper body and arms, and I could also extend my fingers. After spending a lot of time in physical therapy, it became possible for me to grasp a pen.

I've always loved to draw. When I was a kid, I made pictures of everything from Daffy Duck (one of my lifelong role models) to caricatures of my teachers and friends. I've always been a people watcher, it seems; and I've always looked at the world in a sort of skewed way. Everything I see just happens to translate immediately into humor. And so, humor has become my way of coping. As the years have gone by, I have developed a tremendous drive to express my humor by drawing cartoons.

The key to cartooning is to put a different spin on the expected, the normal. And that's one reason why many of my cartoons deal with the disabled: amputees, quadriplegics, paraplegics, the blind. The public is not used to seeing them in cartoons.

But there's another reason why my subjects are often disabled men and women. I'm sick and tired of people who presume to speak for the disabled. Call me a cripple, call me a gimp, call me paralyzed for life.

Just don't call me something I'm not. I'm not "differently abled," and my cartoons show that disabled people should not be treated any differently than anyone else.

All of the men, women, and children who are profiled in the Great Achievers series share this in common: their various handicaps have not prevented them from accomplishing great things. Their life stories are worth knowing about because they have found the strength and courage to develop their talents and to follow their dreams as fully as they can.

Whether able-bodied or disabled, a person must strive to overcome obstacles. There's nothing greater than to see a person who faces challenges and conquers them, regardless of his or her limitations.

Helen Keller (left) and teacher Anne Sullivan converse in 1890 using the manual alphabet. Blind and deaf since the age of 19 months, Helen later explained that she had lived in a "no-world" until Sullivan arrived on March 3, 1887. On that day, she said, it "was my soul's birthday."

1

A Meeting of Minds

THE FIST OF 6-year-old Helen Keller found its mark on Anne Sullivan's mouth, and the 20-year-old teacher's two front teeth landed upon the cottage floor. As she applied a cold compress to her mouth, she remembered expecting her new pupil to be "pale, delicate, and timid." Despite her misconceptions about Helen, Sullivan would not give up on her young student. She had traveled more than 1,000 miles to try to teach Helen, who had been blind, deaf, and mute since the age of 19 months. No stranger to adversity herself, Sullivan was not about to allow the loss of her two front teeth to send her packing.

Although Helen did not realize it at the time, the willful child had met her match in Anne Sullivan. Blind, deaf, and "dumb" (the accepted term of the era for people lacking the ability to speak), Helen was not stupid. Frustrated by her physical limitations, her behavior worsened as she grew. Once she locked her mother in the pantry for hours, smiling gleefully as she stood against the door, feeling the vibrations from her mother's pounding. Such a mischievous scheme required a degree of intelligence, but Helen later said her life had merely been an existence "without hope, anticipation, wonder, faith, or joy." She described herself as "a phantom living in a no-world," consisting of tactile sensations, vibrations, and scents, a prisoner locked in a world of despair.

Deeply frustrated by their failure to help Helen, Mr. and Mrs. Keller had hired Anne Sullivan as a teacher for their daughter. Mrs. Keller and her stepson James met Miss Sullivan at the train station on March 3, 1887. Helen sensed an excitement in the household that day, even though she did not understand what was happening. As the carriage approached the Keller home, the young teacher spotted Helen on the front steps. The image of the girl's rumpled hair, a soiled dress, and black shoes tied with white strings imprinted itself in Anne's memory. Despite Helen's disheveled appearance, Sullivan noticed that she was a very pretty child.

When the carriage came to a stop, Helen dashed down the steps and ran straight into Sullivan. Her busy fingers eagerly explored the young woman's face as she sought to "see" the stranger. But when Sullivan tried to kiss the child, Helen pushed her away with such force that Sullivan almost fell. Grabbing Sullivan's purse, Helen frantically ran her hands along the surface of the locked handbag until her busy fingers found the keyhole. Tugging Sullivan's sleeve, she gestured for her to turn the key.

"She must be very intelligent! That was very clever of her," Sullivan told Mrs. Keller.

"Do you think so?" Kate Keller responded hopefully.

Very few people had ever expressed the belief that Helen was bright. In fact, relatives described her as a wild beast who should be put away. Helen had been a normal child until she developed a high fever at the age of 19 months. The high temperature damaged her brain, leaving her blind and deaf. Soon she forgot the few words that she had spoken as a toddler.

Although the Kellers had failed to help their daughter, they refused to institutionalize her. Instead, they turned to Anne Sullivan to release Helen from her dark inner prison.

As Mrs. Keller led Sullivan to her room on that early spring day, Helen followed them. Helen believed the teacher's purse held food and persisted in trying to open it. Sullivan sensed the child's hunger and steered her new pupil to her trunk, which contained candy. She placed one of Helen's hands on the trunk and the other on her own hand as she mimed an eating motion. Attempting to communicate, Helen had devised her own form of sign language and she easily comprehended such gestures. Sullivan rewarded her new student with the sweets.

Anne Sullivan immediately liked the Keller family. She saw that Captain Arthur Keller, a retired Confederate army officer, was a kind father and deeply loved his young wife, Kate, who was only a few years older than Sullivan. The Kellers also had an infant daughter, Mildred, and two sons from Captain Keller's first marriage: James, who was in his early twenties, and Simpson, who was in his teens.

Despite Sullivan's initial positive feelings about the Kellers upon her arrival, she was startled by the scene she witnessed at breakfast the following morning. During the meal, Helen roamed freely from person to person, examining the contents of each family member's plate, grabbing food, and cramming it into her mouth with her fingers. Feeling pity for Helen, the Kellers allowed her to have her way and became greatly distressed whenever she cried. If Helen did not get what she wanted, she threw violent tantrums that grew in frequency as she became increasingly frustrated over her inability to effectively express herself. Viney, the Kellers' servant, informed Sullivan that force was usually required in managing Helen's most routine tasks, such as combing her hair or fastening her shoes.

This image of Helen as a quiet and neatly dressed seven-year-old posing with a pet dog at her home in Tuscumbia, Alabama, contradicted her true behavior before Sullivan's arrival. Viney, the Kellers' servant, had to use physical force to comb Helen's hair and to dress her because she had a violent temper.

Sullivan immediately recognized the futility of such permissiveness and considered the family's attitude to be Helen's greatest obstacle. Sullivan resolved that she would teach Helen how to behave in a civilized manner. She was, however, acutely sensitive to the fact that she was regarded as a newcomer in the Keller household. She realized that changes would have to be implemented gradually and diplomatically if she were to succeed without antagonizing the family. Although Sullivan understood the challenge of taming her charge, she also saw great promise in Helen.

While she was a student at the Perkins Institution in Boston, Massachusetts, Anne Sullivan had mastered the manual alphabet, a system devised in Spain by a Trappist monk who had taken the vow of silence. It consisted of letters formed with the fingers, and a blind and deaf person could read the letters by touching the hand of the individual who recreated the words one letter at a time. Sullivan had become friendly with a longtime resident of Perkins named Laura Bridgman, who had been blind and deaf since the age of two. Through her lifelong friendship with Laura, Sullivan gained great insights into the unique world of blind, deaf, and mute people.

The students at Perkins had given Sullivan a doll they had made for Helen as a gift, and the new teacher offered the present to the child after breakfast. As she felt the doll, Helen's face beamed with delight. Immediately, Sullivan took Helen's hand and spelled *d-o-l-l*. Captivated by the touch of Sullivan's fingers, Helen revealed by her expression that some cognitive process was taking place. To reinforce the message, Sullivan made the sign that Helen had devised to indicate she could keep an object and the child clutched the doll to her chest with glee. Sullivan immediately spelled *d-o-l-l* into Helen's hand again. She then offered her own palm to the child. Amazed, she watched Helen's slim fingers slowly spell *d-o-l-l* in her teacher's hand. Sullivan, elated by her student's response, then made a tactical mistake. She tried to take the doll away from Helen for a moment. Helen immediately launched into a violent rage. Sullivan had never before witnessed such a tantrum—her young charge flailed her body, kicked, and pounded her fists on the floor. When she cried, Helen's weak vocal chords produced an oddly pitched wail.

Fearing that she had destroyed Helen's initial trust, Sullivan raced to the kitchen and asked Viney for a small cake. Returning to Helen, she held the cake under the girl's nose. Helen sniffed the fragrant pastry and when she attempted to grab the cake, Sullivan gently took her hand and spelled *c-a-k-e* in her palm. Once again, Helen's face registered the same thoughtful expression that she had displayed earlier about the doll. Helen quickly traced the letters *c-a-k-e* in her teacher's hand and was promptly rewarded with a slice of cake, which she eagerly devoured.

Again Sullivan formed the letters *d-o-l-l* in Helen's hand. At once, Helen spelled *d-o-l* in Sullivan's hand. The teacher took Helen's hand and added the missing *l*. She then gave the doll to the child, who clutched it to her heart as she ran from the room. Although Helen would have nothing more to do with her new teacher for the remainder of the day, Anne Sullivan felt triumphant. In less than 24 hours she had penetrated the mysterious realm of Helen's mind, and she could see the potential her student possessed in learning to effectively communicate with others.

Sullivan's next major challenge took place at the breakfast table a few days after her arrival. As usual, Helen walked around the table, investigating the contents of each person's plate with her hands and grabbing whatever she wanted. No one objected to this intrusion; the family members ignored her and carried on their conversation. When Helen tried to snatch food from Sullivan's plate, the teacher pushed her hands aside. Helen scowled and angrily pinched Sullivan's arm. Sullivan then slapped Helen's hand. Screaming in her strange-sounding voice, Helen grabbed for Sullivan's plate, but for her efforts got her hand firmly slapped again. The family watched in horror. Finally, Mrs. Keller stood in silence and left the dining room. The rest of the family filed out behind her. Sullivan locked the door behind them, leaving her alone with Helen.

Although Sullivan's appetite was gone, she forced herself to continue eating her breakfast. Lying on the floor, Helen shrieked and kicked, and attempted to yank Sullivan's chair away from the table with all her might. After failing to unseat Sullivan, Helen stopped crying and stood up to discover what Sullivan was doing. Determining that

Sullivan was eating, Helen once again grabbed for her teacher's food. Sullivan delivered another strong smack to Helen's hand. Finding nobody else in the room, Helen returned to her seat and began to eat her own food with her hands. Next, Sullivan placed a spoon in Helen's hand and filled it with food. The child violently hurled the spoon across the room and food flew through the air. Sullivan pulled Helen from her chair and dragged the flailing girl to the spot where the spoon had landed. Sullivan forced her to pick up the spoon, then lugged the fighting, howling child back to her seat, planted her on the chair, and tried to push a spoonful of food into Helen's mouth. Every time Sullivan stuck the spoon in Helen's hand it landed on the floor, until Helen's hunger finally overcame her stubbornness and she began shoveling the food into her mouth. Exhausted, she quietly finished her breakfast, but the battle had not ended.

Sullivan showed Helen how to fold her napkin and place it on the table. But each time it was handed to her, Helen threw the linen cloth upon the floor. Repeating her earlier strategy, Sullivan stuck to her guns until Helen finally yielded and the napkin was folded and placed on the table. Sullivan knew the fight was not over, but she felt she had won the first round.

Later, Sullivan wrote to Sophia Hopkins, a Perkins staff member and a longtime friend, "I suppose I shall have many such battles with the little woman before she learns two essential things I can teach her, obedience and love."

By this time, Helen viewed Anne Sullivan as a curious adversary. Feeling herself to be in an undeclared war, she locked Sullivan in her room and hid the key. Captain Keller had to hoist a ladder to Sullivan's window so that she could leave the room. Sullivan understood that she and Helen would have to have a meeting of the minds. Asserting her position as Helen's teacher, Sullivan insisted that she and her student be allowed to live alone in a small cottage near the house for two weeks. Helen's parents were skeptical about the arrangement, but they feared losing Sullivan as Helen's teacher and reluctantly agreed to the plan.

During the first two hours in the cottage, a ceaseless battle was waged in which Helen kicked and screamed herself into a state of exhaustion. Sullivan later described the scene: "I never saw such strength and endurance in a child. But fortunately for us both, I am a little stronger, and quite as obstinate when I set out."

After two weeks, a state of peace existed in the little cottage. Although Helen dutifully retraced the spelling of words in her teacher's hand, it was obvious that the motions had no meaning to the child. The breakthrough that Sullivan had hoped and prayed for finally occurred on April 5, 1887. Sullivan sent the following report to Perkins.

This morning, while she was washing, she wanted to know the name for "water." . . . I spelled "w-a-t-e-r" and thought no more about it until after breakfast. . . . We went out to

On April 5, 1887, Helen finally understood the concept of language at this water pump when Teacher spelled w-a-t-e-r into one of Helen's hands while she filled a mug with water from the spout. Years later, reflecting on that moment, Keller wrote: "It was as if I had come back to life after being dead."

the pump house, and I made Helen hold her mug under the spout while I pumped. As the cold water gushed forth, filling the mug, I spelled "w-a-t-e-r" into Helen's free hand. The word coming so close upon the sensation of cold water rushing over her hand seemed to startle her. She dropped the mug and stood as one transfixed. A new light came over her face. She spelled "w-a-t-e-r" several times. Then she dropped on the ground and asked for its name and pointed to the pump and the trellis, and suddenly turning around she asked for my name. I spelled 'Teacher.'

Helen later described the scene in her 1903 autobiography, *The Story of My Life*: "Someone was drawing water, and my teacher placed my hand under the spout. As the cold stream gushed over one hand, she spelled into the other the word *water,* first slowly, then rapidly. I stood still, my whole attention fixed upon the motions of her fingers. Suddenly I felt a misty consciousness as of something forgotten—a thrill of returning thought; and somehow the mystery of language was revealed to me." Commenting further, she said, "It was as if I had come back to life after being dead. . . ."

Although Helen Keller's date of birth was June 27, 1880, she later said that the day Anne Sullivan arrived at her house "was my soul's birthday." Sullivan had freed Helen from the seemingly inescapable bondage in which she had existed for most of her young life. From Helen's rebirth at the water pump, these two people, student and teacher, would go on to become the world's most renowned living examples of the boundless power of the human spirit to overcome physical challenges—as well as certain demands imposed by society at the time—with dignity and grace.

After Helen learned the manual alphabet her fingers never stopped spelling words.
She often talked to herself by spelling in her own hand and, as seen in this photograph,
she even practiced on Jumbo, the Kellers' pet Irish setter.

2

LIVING IN
A "NO-WORLD"

HELEN ADAMS KELLER was born in Tuscumbia, Alabama, on June 27, 1880. The first child of Kate Adams Keller and Captain Arthur Keller, Helen was a joy to her parents. Captain Keller, a wealthy landowner and newspaper publisher, came from a distinguished southern family and the Kellers resided in a comfortable home, constructed of Georgia pine and covered with English ivy. Known as Ivy Green, the isolated, vine-covered house featured winding staircases, stately columns, and numerous outbuildings. It sat opposite a house once owned by President Andrew Jackson.

Captain Keller had distinguished himself for the Confederacy in the Civil War and returned from the conflict to become a prominent citizen of Tuscumbia, owning and editing his own weekly newspaper, the *North Alabamian*. An avid sportsman, Keller was known for his fine hunting dogs. He and his friends would gather at his mountaintop

Arthur Keller, Helen's father, served with distinction as a captain in the Confederate army. After the Civil War, he returned to Tuscumbia and edited his own weekly news-paper, the North Alabamian.

summer camp, where they exchanged stories on a wide porch surrounded by evergreens and persimmons. Following the death of his first wife, Keller married Kate Adams. Kate, 20 years younger than her husband, shared his love of country living. While Captain Keller worked in his newspaper office in town, she tended the pigs, turkeys, chickens, and sheep that roamed the spacious grounds. Kate Keller especially enjoyed her old-fashioned garden and was known throughout the county for curing delicious country hams.

Helen was born in a little house next to Ivy Green. Kate wished to name her baby daughter "Helen Everett," after her cousin Edward Everett Hale, author of the short story "The Man Without a Country," but rushing to church, Arthur Keller incorrectly reported the baby's name as "Helen Adams," inserting Kate's maiden name instead. The blue-eyed infant quickly developed a warm, outgoing personality that enchanted everyone around her. A born mimic, Helen easily imitated gestures and words to the delight of her parents. Helen's father insisted that at the age of six months Helen could say "How do you do?" and her favorite word, "wah-wah" for *water*.

On her first birthday, Helen took her first steps as she toddled from her mother's lap to grab a sunbeam. Captain Keller fondly recalled returning home each evening to his precocious daughter, who ran gleefully to her father and kissed him. Helen's days were filled with wonderful discoveries. She took great pleasure in playing games such as hide-and-seek with her mother, hiding behind the huge boxwood hedge. Mrs. Keller later told Helen that she had had the most wonderfully keen eyesight, finding buttons and needles unnoticed by others. At age 12, Helen wrote, "The beginning of my life was very simple and very much like the beginning of every other little life."

On a cold February day in 1882, Helen suddenly became ill with an extremely high fever. The doctor's diagnosis was "acute congestion of the stomach and brain," and the prognosis was death. When the fever quickly subsided and it was apparent that Helen would survive, the Kellers immediately rejoiced over their daughter's miraculous recovery. The day after the fever broke, however, Mrs. Keller noticed that Helen did not blink when she passed her hand in front of her daughter's eyes. As the days passed, Mrs. Keller observed that if she shouted, Helen showed no reaction. Although Helen's life was spared, the fever had permanently damaged her brain, forever destroying her ability to see or hear.

"I was too young to realize what had happened," Helen later explained. "When I awoke and found that all was dark and still, I suppose I thought it was night and I must have wondered why day was so long in coming. Gradually, however, I got used to the silence and darkness that surrounded me, and forgot that it ever had been day. Soon even my childish voice was stilled because I had ceased to hear any sound."

Helen sank into deep despair that she later compared to a state of anarchy (chaos). Feeling helpless and alone, she likened herself to a ship groping its way through a dense fog at sea. "But all was not lost," Helen later wrote. "After all, sight and hearing are but two of the most beautiful blessings which God has given me. The most precious, the most wonderful of His gifts was still mine. My mind remained clear and active."

In the 1880s, little was understood about severe physical disabilities. Hardly 100 years had passed since the world's first school for the blind had been established in Paris, France, in 1784. Individuals with Helen's condition were considered by many to be idiots, possessing no capacity for thought or feelings. Kate Keller's brother, Fred Adams, urged his sister to institutionalize Helen. "You really ought to put that child away, Kate," he wrote, "she is mentally defective, and it is not pleasant to see her about." Indeed, to visitors and servants, Helen often appeared to be unmanageable. Frustrated when others could not comprehend her

Kate Adams, a reigning beauty in Memphis, Tennessee, was 20 years younger than Arthur Keller when they married. Mrs. Keller loved to play hide-and-seek with her first daughter, Helen, and later told her that before her debilitating fever, Helen had had very keen eyesight.

gesture ↓

gestures, she would lie on the floor, pound her fists, kick her feet, and wail until she was exhausted.

Nevertheless, the Kellers considered Helen's attempts at mimicry to be an indication of high intelligence. If she desired a piece of cake, she developed a gesture of beating the batter; bread was signed by making the motions of spreading butter and slicing. If she wanted ice cream, she imitated the turning of the ice cream freezer's crank and then hugged herself to make a shivering motion. As Helen grew and her vocabulary of signs expanded, her parents hoped that something could be done to rehabilitate their daughter. Although they knew of the Perkins Institution in Boston, they were reluctant to send their young daughter to any facility so far from Alabama.

In 1886, Kate Keller read Charles Dickens's *American Notes.* The acclaimed English author had written the travel book during a visit to America; it was published in 1842. In his detailed travelogue, Dickens described his visit to Perkins, America's first school for the blind. "It stands a mile or two without the town, a cheerful, healthy spot; and is an airy, spacious, handsome edifice. It is built upon a height, commanding a harbor." There he met Bostonian

Helen was born in this small cottage next to Ivy Green. She had a warm, outgoing personality as a baby and effortlessly mimicked gestures and words to the delight of her family.

Dr. Samuel Gridley Howe. Howe received his degree in medicine from Harvard University in 1824, and after spending six years in Greece as a surgeon he returned to Massachusetts, where he immediately dedicated himself to humane causes and to helping people who were less fortunate than he. In 1831, Howe was appointed director of the New England Asylum for the Blind (renamed the Perkins Institution and later the Perkins School for the Blind). A compassionate person, Howe often walked the halls at Perkins blindfolded to develop more empathy for the obstacles that the blind students faced in the corridors.

One of Howe's most outstanding contributions to the education of the blind was his press for printing books in the braille alphabet. Braille, a raised-dot system of writing, was invented by the Frenchman Louis Braille in the early 1820s. Prior to Howe's braille press, very few books for the blind existed. Printed in what became known as "Howe type," these works included a geography text he wrote for the blind and the first atlas with raised maps.

Howe became most famous for his work at Perkins with Laura Bridgman, the blind, deaf, and mute student who later befriended Anne Sullivan. Howe admitted that prior to instructing seven-year-old Laura he too believed the blind to have impaired intellectual abilities. Howe's experience in teaching Laura opened his mind to the possibilities of educating individuals with multiple sensory impairments. Describing the relationship between Howe and Bridgman, Dickens wrote that the doctor had saved his student from a darkness and stillness "as profound as that of a closed tomb at midnight."

Like Laura Bridgman, Helen possessed an endless curiosity about her environment and had thoughts and emotions like any other human being. Once, when she was jealous of her baby sister, Mildred, Helen attempted to upset the infant's cradle. In another incident, Helen, curious about scissors, cut off a playmate's curls. Another time, when she was in a frolicsome spirit, she poured oil

Laura Bridgman, the first known deaf and blind person to be educated, went to study at the Perkins Institution for the Blind when she was seven. The Kellers first learned of Bridgman—who lost her sight, hearing, smell, and taste after an attack of scarlet fever at the age of two—after reading Charles Dickens's American Notes, *in which the English author described meeting her at Perkins.*

on her own head, patted her face with powder, and dressed up in a bustle and a lace veil. Then there was the time she realized the drying effects of fire and attempted to dry her wet apron in front of the fire, setting the apron ablaze when she got too close to the flames.

In 1886, the Kellers took their daughter to meet Dr. Chisholm, a Baltimore, Maryland, oculist (eye doctor). The trip to Baltimore was Helen's first long train ride. It was an arduous journey for the restless child; to help pass the time, she strung seashells on a string and played with the conductor's coattails as he walked through the car punching tickets. When her gifted fingers discovered that the homemade doll accompanying her on the trip had no eyes, Helen gestured the message to her mother, who understood and, to Helen's delight, immediately made button eyes for the doll.

Like the other doctors the Kellers consulted, Chisholm offered no hope for restoring Helen's sight. However, he suggested that the effects of Helen's sensory impairments could be lessened through proper care and training. Chisholm referred the Kellers to Dr. Alexander Graham Bell, the Scottish-born inventor and teacher of deaf-mutes, who lived in nearby Washington, D.C. Bell's interest in the deaf was multifaceted. Both his mother and his wife were deaf. His father had become a pioneer in deaf education, inventing a system of phonetics instruction called "visible speech," which consisted of a code of symbols that indicated the position of the throat, tongue, and lips in making sounds. These symbols guided the deaf in learning to speak. Bell continued his father's work and attempted to record the vibrations of the voice visibly on a sheet of soot-covered glass to aid deaf students in "seeing" sounds. One of Bell's inventions—the telephone—was a by-product of his phonetics system.

Helen clearly remembered her first meeting with Bell. Holding her on his knee, Bell allowed the six-year-old to examine his watch. "He made it strike for me," Helen later

wrote. "He understood my signs and I knew it and immediately loved him." Bell suggested that Mrs. Keller write
to Howe's successor at Perkins, Howe's son-in-law, Michael Anagnos.

When Kate Keller's letter reached Anagnos in Boston,
Anagnos was struck by the similarities between Laura
Bridgman and Helen Keller. He immediately wrote to the
Kellers, offering encouragement that a teacher could be
found for their daughter. He felt he knew just the right
person for the position.

Born in 1866 to illiterate potato-famine refugees from
Limerick, Ireland, Anne Mansfield Sullivan had con-
tracted trachoma at age two. Trachoma, a chronic infec-
tious disease of the inner surface of the eyelids and the
cornea, was once thought to be caused by a virus but is
now believed to be caused by a strain of bacteria. The
disease is prevalent in hot and dry areas that have little
water or poor hygienic conditions. The trachoma caused
hard lumps to form inside Annie's eyelids, scratching and
scarring the eyeballs, and she nearly became blind. When
his wife died, Mr. Sullivan sent 10-year-old Annie and her
younger brother, Jamie, to the poorhouse in Tewksbury,
Massachusetts, and the siblings lived among the inmates,
who included orphans, alcoholics, the elderly, and the
insane. Jamie died in childhood at Tewksbury. Annie had
two eye operations performed on her to alleviate the effects of trachoma while she lived at Tewksbury, but they
did little to improve her vision. Later surgery, however,
restored some of her eyesight.

Sullivan's future appeared bleak, but she possessed an
unusually resilient spirit and she dreamed of receiving an
education that would free her from the bondage of poverty
and despair. When a committee from the Massachusetts
State Board of Charities visited Tewksbury to investigate
conditions at the institution, they happened upon 14-year-
old Annie. Bolting from the other inmates, Annie ran up
to the officials and blurted, "I want to go to school."

Helen reads Anne Sullivan's lips by feeling the vibration and position of her mouth and lips. While she was still at Perkins, Sullivan, who had trachoma and had nearly lost her eyesight as a child, prepared to teach Helen by studying Samuel Gridley Howe's detailed files on his work with Laura Bridgman.

Leaving the poorhouse that day, the committee chairman, R. F. Sanborn, was haunted by the young girl's plea. He immediately inquired about Annie and arranged to have her sent to the Perkins Institution.

In 1880, Perkins was the best such school in the nation. Only the children of wealthy New England parents attended the facility, and Annie was the sole charity case in the school. Her resolute character and willingness to voice her convictions helped her survive, although some faculty members viewed her as impudent and wanted her expelled. Her friendship with the 50-year-old Laura Bridgman was a great source of strength and inspiration to Annie during those lonely years at Perkins.

As the valedictorian of the class of 1886, Sullivan addressed the commencement audience, saying, "And now we are going out into the busy world to take our share of life's burdens, and do our little to make the world better, wiser, and happier."

When Anagnos approached Annie Sullivan about the teaching position that the Kellers offered, the young woman initially felt apprehensive about living in the Deep

South. Sullivan realized that northerners, or "Yankees," were still regarded with suspicion in the South, the Civil War having ended only 22 years earlier. She concluded, however, that no experience could be more horrific than her early years at the Tewksbury poorhouse. Sitting in her quiet room at Perkins, she recalled how, prior to her brother's death, to be alone together, the two often spent time in the institution's "deadhouse," a rat- and cockroach-infested room at the end of their ward where patients who had died were taken on a metal cart. As Sullivan grappled with such frightening memories, she could almost hear the clanging sound of the metal cart removing another body from the ward.

Although Anne Sullivan welcomed the challenge of teaching Helen, she doubted her abilities to perform such a task adequately. But she also realized that it was time to leave Perkins. She was no longer a student, and she had no money, no family, and no place to go. The teaching position paid $25 per month and gave her the opportunity to help another individual.

Sullivan immediately began preparing to teach her new pupil. Despite the intense strain placed upon her weak eyes, Sullivan spent six months studying Howe's extensive files on his work with Laura Bridgman. She immersed herself in Howe's theory and practice, but she also brought the perspective of more modern methods to the applications of Howe's accomplishments, which were performed 50 years earlier.

Sophia Hopkins, a Perkins staff member and Sullivan's confidante, helped the young teacher to acquire a modest wardrobe of remade clothing, and Anagnos loaned her money for her train fare to Tuscumbia. On a cold Boston morning in March 1887, with her eyes still swollen and sore from another recent operation to improve her vision, the 20-year-old Sullivan, dressed in a gray suit, set out on the longest and most profound journey of her young life.

Alexander Graham Bell (left) hands the string of his kite to Helen so that she is able to feel the pull of the kite as it soars above them. After their meeting with President Cleveland in Washington, D.C., Helen, Sullivan, and Mrs. Keller visited Bell, a prominent teacher of the deaf, who had been following Helen's progress very closely.

3

"I THINK"

WHEN ANNE SULLIVAN arrived at the Keller home on March 3, 1887, she found the six-year-old Helen spoiled, pampered, and out of control. In just two weeks, she had succeeded in taming her young charge and gaining her trust. The young teacher recorded the fascinating events of her trials and triumphs with Helen and the Keller family in detailed reports to Anagnos and in letters to her friend Sophia at Perkins. With each passing day, Sullivan's confidence grew. In a letter to Hopkins dated March 20, 1887, Sullivan wrote:

> My heart is singing for joy this morning! The light of understanding has shone upon my little pupil, and behold all things are changed!
>
> The wild creature of two weeks ago has been transformed into a gentle child. She is sitting beside me as I write, serene and happy, crocheting a long red chain of Scotch wool. . . . She lets me kiss her now, and when she is in a particularly gentle mood, she will sit in my lap. . . . The great

step—the step that counts—has been taken. The little savage has learned her first lesson in obedience. Already people remark the difference in Helen. Her father looks in on us morning and evening, and sees her contentedly stringing her beads and sewing, and exclaims, "How quiet she is!" When I first came her movements were so insistent that one always felt there was something unnatural and weird about her.

The next morning, Sullivan added this postscript: "Last night when I got in bed, Helen stole into my arms of her own accord and kissed me for the first time, and I thought my heart would burst, so full was it of joy."

Helen and Sullivan returned to the main house, the child bursting to learn. "Everything had a name and each name gave birth to a new thought," Helen later wrote, "every object which I touched seemed to quiver with life." Immediately, Helen wanted to know the name for everything: nouns like *door, bed, candy,* and *baby,* and verbs, such as *run, sit, walk, go, come,* and *give.* It was as if her mind was soaking up six years of learning in one day. By the time Helen went to sleep that night, she had learned 30 new words.

The entire Keller household was amazed by Helen's transformation. Everyone watched in wonder as Helen's deft fingers moved ceaselessly, spelling words. It was an especially touching moment for Sullivan when Helen climbed into her mother's lap and spelled *m-o-t-h-e-r* on Mrs. Keller's hand.

By April 5, 1887, the day of her "rebirth" at the water pump and just 32 days after Sullivan's arrival, Helen was able to communicate with others, express herself, ask questions, and receive answers.

Although Helen was Sullivan's pupil, Anne was in the infancy of her teaching experience. She too was learning each day, and her willingness to discover the most effective means of instructing Helen greatly enhanced her success. Always searching for further insights into language acquisition, Sullivan experienced a revelation as she sat in the garden with Helen's 15-month-old cousin one day. The young teacher observed that although the child could not speak, she understood what was being said to her. She gave the little girl a set of commands, such as "Touch your ear" and "Take the flower to your mother." Even though the toddler could not say the words, she clearly comprehended their meaning. This knowledge greatly shaped Sullivan's philosophy in teaching Helen. If children learned words long before they could speak, she would immerse Helen in words. The words would come first, and the understanding would follow. Sullivan based her entire teaching method with Helen on this premise.

Only a generation earlier, Samuel Gridley Howe had said, "A teacher cannot be a child," but Sullivan concluded that a teacher must be a child, eager to demonstrate and share the spontaneous joys of unending learning. Instead of rigid classroom sessions, Sullivan took her student into the world to explore and discover everything around them.

Each spring morning the two were out the door, eagerly examining trees, butterflies, birds, plants, and animals in the beautiful Alabama weather. Sullivan, whom Helen called Teacher, and her student sauntered down old cow paths, climbed trees, examined seed pods, and hunted for persimmons. Each moment represented new discoveries and new words—always new words for Helen.

By not planning formal lessons, Sullivan allowed spontaneous experiences to shape her instruction. One morning, Sullivan was dressing in her room when an excited Helen burst through the door. At first, Helen spelled *d-o-g* and *b-a-b-y* repeatedly in Sullivan's palm. Next, she held up five fingers and then began to suck on each one. Sullivan could not imagine what her eager student was attempting to explain. She feared that Helen's younger sister, Mildred, had been injured by a dog and yet the happy expression on her pupil's face assured her that nothing was wrong. Encouraging her teacher to hurry,

Helen led Sullivan to the wellhouse where she found that one of the family's dogs had given birth to five new puppies.

Sullivan instantly taught Helen two new words: *five* and *puppy*. Helen observed that one of the puppies, the runt of the litter, was much smaller than the others. Helen spelled *s-m-a-l-l* in her teacher's hand. Sullivan responded by spelling *v-e-r-y s-m-a-l-l* in Helen's hand. Such concepts fascinated Helen and she eagerly applied her new knowledge. As they returned to the house, Helen picked up stones to reinforce her understanding. She showed Sullivan that one stone was small and another very small. Touching Mildred, Helen spelled *b-a-b-y small* and *p-u-p-p-y—very small*. It seemed as if Helen's fingers never stopped spelling words. Not only did she talk to herself by spelling in her own hand, she even spelled words on the family dog's paw.

By the end of May, Helen had mastered 300 new words. She quickly moved from the use of single words to phrases and sentences. Sullivan felt that Helen was ready to learn to read. She began the instruction by introducing Helen to the raised alphabet. She spelled each letter in her student's hand and then had Helen trace the same letter on raised cardboard alphabet cards that she had brought with her from Perkins. This technique made it possible for Helen to read with her fingertips. Helen easily mastered the entire alphabet in one day and was able to read all the words that she had previously learned. Next, Sullivan introduced sentence frames; using this device, Helen could arrange words in any way she chose. Finally, Sullivan shared with Helen the simple raised-letter books that she had brought from Perkins.

True to Sullivan's predictions, her young pupil read easily and could not get enough of the few books that her teacher had in her possession. One morning, Sullivan discovered that Helen had taken one of the books to bed with her. When Teacher questioned her student about the

There are two worlds: the world that we can measure with line and rule, and the world that we feel with our heart and imagination.

Helen Keller

book, Helen responded, "Book afraid—cry much. Girl not afraid. Book sleep with girl." Sullivan wrote to Perkins requesting personalized word cards for Helen with the names of Helen's family and the names of things in her environment, such as farm animals and implements. Using her sentence frame, Helen endlessly created new sentences.

Sullivan next taught her eager student to write. Although Helen could not see what she was writing, a writing board enabled her to stay within even horizontal lines so that the words were uniform and legible to others. By guiding her right hand with her left, she reproduced the raised letters that she felt on the alphabet cards. Known as "square-hand" script, this form of writing was taught to students at Perkins.

Helen's first letter was addressed to her cousin Anna on June 17. It included simple sentences, such as "jack will give helen stick of candy" and "helen will write anna." The letter had no punctuation or capital letters, but it was clearly legible. Helen's letters provided visible proof of her achievements and the Keller family relatives admitted that they were impressed with her progress. However, as the intense Alabama heat set in, Helen grew visibly thinner. Although everyone suffered from the effects of the tropical weather, some Keller family members, still suspicious of the Yankee teacher, suggested that Sullivan was pushing her young student too hard. In a letter to Anagnos in which she addressed their criticisms, Sullivan wrote,

After Sullivan taught Helen how to read the raised alphabet, she then taught her how to write in "square-hand" script, a sample of which is shown here. By using a writing board and guiding her right hand with her left, Helen could stay within even horizontal lines, making the words uniform and readable.

"We are bothered a great deal by people who . . . tell us that Helen is overdoing, that her mind is too active (these very people thought she had no mind at all a few months ago!) . . . and they suggest many impossible absurd remedies. But so far, nobody seems to have thought of chloroforming [putting her to sleep using a special liquid] her, which is, I think, the only effective way of stopping the natural exercise of her faculties."

Michael Anagnos was especially proud of Sullivan. Her achievements reflected the excellent training Perkins had given Sullivan and his own good judgment in selecting her. He included Sullivan's letters about Helen in the annual reports of the Perkins Institution. Anagnos described Sullivan as a "genius" who used "originality" in her teaching methods. Although Sullivan appreciated his praise, she grew increasingly concerned about the resulting publicity.

The novice teacher instinctively feared that too much public attention might erode Helen's progress. Writing to Sophia Hopkins, she expressed her great optimism about Helen's promise while relating a fear of impediments to that success: "I want to say something for your ears alone. Something within me tells me I shall succeed beyond my wildest dreams. Were it not for some circumstances that make such an idea highly improbable, even absurd, I should think Helen's education would surpass in interest and wonder Dr. Howe's achievement." Discussing the public's extraordinary interest in a person such as Helen, she added, "You must promise never to show my letters to anyone. My beautiful Helen shall not be transformed into a prodigy [child genius] if I can help it."

Sullivan's experiences as a student at Perkins shaped her strong opposition to any pity toward a blind individual. The students at Perkins were encouraged to be as independent as possible, and this is what Sullivan wanted for her young student as well. Calling pity "the chief stumbling block to the sightless," Sullivan treated Helen as if she were a seeing and hearing individual and never praised her until she had mastered a task. The young teacher saw her mission as guiding Helen to achieve her goals. Helen later remembered that Sullivan had said, "You will be glad when you recall the merciless prodding to which I subjected you."

Louis Braille's raised-dot process of writing is based on a coded system of a six-dot cell with 63 possible arrangements of the dots. In addition to the alphabet, Braille included punctuation marks and numerals in his system, and he later invented a method of writing music. Mastering braille enabled Helen to read what she wrote.

Soon after Helen's seventh birthday, Sullivan began to teach her to read braille. Several forms of braille existed in 1887. In addition to the original raised-dot alphabet developed by Louis Braille in Paris, France, in the 1820s, there were other systems: Boston Line Type, invented by Dr. Howe at Perkins; New York Point, devised by William Bell Wait, Superintendent of the New York School for the Blind; and American Braille, devised by a teacher at Perkins at about the time that Sullivan had entered the institution in 1880. Louis Braille's raised-dot system had gained a wider acceptance than the others and more materials were available in this form. Based on a coded system of a six-dot "cell" (shape), Louis Braille devised 63 possible arrangements of the dots, which included the alphabet, punctuation marks, and numerals. Eventually, Braille expanded his system to include a means of writing music as well. Helen learned to write braille using a stylus, but later a six-key device known as a braillewriter, which was very similar to a typewriter, was introduced, making writing much easier.

Although learning to write in braille was considered a difficult task, requiring many dots to be punched for each letter, Helen easily mastered the skill. Writing in this system enabled her to read what she had written, an impossibility with the square-hand print. Because Sullivan had had little exposure to braille at Perkins, reading and writing in that mode were awkward for her, too, and she was soon struggling to keep up with Helen. When Santa Claus brought her paper and a braille slate at Christmas, Helen was elated. "I will write many letters," she said, "and I will thank Santa Claus very much."

Throughout the winter and spring of 1888, Helen eagerly absorbed everything that Sullivan could teach her. Once, during a family discussion about the national economy, Helen asked Sullivan for an explanation. Teacher spelled, "No, you cannot understand it yet."

"How do you know that I cannot understand?" replied Helen. "I have a good mind!"

As the warm days of spring unfolded, Helen and Sullivan often made their way down to Keller's Landing, an abandoned wharf on the Tennessee River. There, Sullivan formed shapes in the sand using water and pebbles, so Helen's hands could feel the concepts behind words such as *spring, stream, river,* and *dam.* When Helen learned the name of the city Hot Springs, Arkansas, she was intrigued by the idea of hot springs.

"Who made fire under the ground?" she asked Sullivan. "Is it like fire in stove? Does hot water burn roots of plants and trees?" she inquired. Each question seemed to lead to another in Helen's thirst to learn about the universe that had suddenly been revealed to her.

In May 1888, Michael Anagnos extended an invitation for Sullivan and her student to visit Perkins. Sullivan enthusiastically accepted the offer, thrilled at the prospect of Helen being able to visit the wonderful school where her teacher had spent her happiest years. Helen would finally be able to meet Perkins's most celebrated student, Laura Bridgman, and its director, Michael Anagnos.

Later that month, Helen, Sullivan, and Mrs. Keller boarded a Boston-bound train. Helen was ecstatic that she would have the opportunity to meet other blind children. She had also received invitations to visit Alexander Graham Bell and President Grover Cleveland at a stop in Washington, D.C. During the trip, Sullivan's fingers ceaselessly tapped out words in Helen's hand like a telegraph machine as she described the Tennessee River, meadows, rolling hills, many types of trees, grazing cows, and sheep. Arriving in the nation's capital, the trio first visited Bell. Although he had corresponded with Helen and was aware of her progress, the eminent educator of the deaf was amazed to actually witness her accomplishments. "Her achievement is without parallel in the education of

In 1893, Sullivan teaches Helen using the manual alphabet. Helen looked forward to her visit at Perkins, where for the first time she could communicate with other children using the manual alphabet.

the deaf," Bell exclaimed. At the White House, President Cleveland warmly greeted the well-known child whom he had asked to meet. "He was very glad to see me," Helen later wrote.

Helen's joy in meeting the blind children at Perkins exceeded her expectations. For the first time, she could communicate with a group of other children through the manual alphabet. "It delighted me inexpressibly to find that they knew the manual alphabet," she later said. The students described the school to Helen and she enthusiastically joined them in their games. Perkins boasted the largest collection of materials for the blind in the United States and Helen felt as though she were in heaven as she discovered the bounty of books, running her fingers over their pages.

Kate Keller's favorite memory of the visit involved Helen's identification of a gadget, a strange-looking mechanism whose function no one else could understand. Helen felt the gadget carefully with her gifted hands, and her face lit up. She quickly spelled *l-e-m-o-n-a-d-e* in Teacher's hand. Suddenly, it was obvious to everyone that the contraption was indeed a new type of lemon-squeezer.

"How did you know?" Mrs. Keller asked her daughter.

"I think," Helen answered triumphantly.

Sullivan wanted Helen to meet the 58-year-old Laura Bridgman, who had been blind, deaf, and mute since the age of two. Sullivan had been Bridgman's friend for years at Perkins. The older woman immediately recognized the young teacher merely by the feel of her fingers.

Whenever Helen was introduced to a stranger, she felt the person's face with her fingers, enabling her to envision the individual. However, when Helen touched Bridgman's face after meeting her, the older woman cautioned, "You must not be forward when calling on a lady." Undeterred, Helen asked to examine her crocheted lace, but Bridgman snapped, "I'm afraid your hands are not clean." Helen later described her meeting with Bridgman, recounting, "To me, she seemed like a statue I had once felt in a garden. She was so motionless and her hands were so cool, like flowers that had grown in shady places."

Although Bridgman demonstrated much promise as Dr. Howe's young student, she had never adapted well to the world outside the institution and had chosen to remain within its walls where she often sat in her room crocheting. Howe had recognized Bridgman's cool nature and had described her as jealous and condescending. In contrast, Sullivan knew that Helen possessed special qualities. "There is something about her that attracts everyone . . . her joyous interest in everybody and everything." Sullivan hoped Helen would embrace the world and knew her student's warm, outgoing personality could eventually spread a message of hope and inspiration around the world.

Helen (center) and Alexander Graham Bell (far right) exchange reactions to an excursion with Sullivan (bottom left) and two friends. Bell believed that Helen should be exposed to all the experiences of a normal child; consequently, he sponsored several trips for her, including one to Niagara Falls.

4

"I Must Speak"

WHEN THE SPRING SEMESTER ended at Perkins in June 1888, Helen and Mrs. Keller accompanied Sullivan on a visit to her friend, Sophia Hopkins, on Cape Cod, Massachusetts, where they spent the summer months. It was the first time Helen had ever experienced the ocean. As she joyously splashed in the waves for the first time, she asked the others, "Who put salt in the water?"

The trio returned to Tuscumbia in the fall, tanned, rejuvenated, and eager to resume Helen's studies. During the winter of 1888–89, however, Sullivan's weak eyes began to bother her once again, necessitating a return to Boston for surgery. To avoid being separated from Helen, she arranged for the two of them to stay at Perkins, where Sullivan could continue teaching Helen during her recovery.

Although Helen was never officially enrolled as a student at Perkins, she and Teacher spent the next four winters there at the invitation of Anagnos, returning to Alabama when the school closed each summer. At Perkins, Helen was exposed to a variety of instructional experi-

Helen (standing at left) poses with other Perkins students, including Tommy Stringer (lower right), for whom Helen had raised tuition money. Helen had a warm and compassionate personality, and throughout her life she reached out to others who needed assistance.

ences. She enjoyed modeling clay, studied French, and persuaded Anagnos to teach her his native language, Greek. Sullivan was still responsible for Helen's education, but her student had the benefit of being taught by other faculty members as well. Nevertheless, Sullivan was the only one who could keep pace with Helen's amazing rate of fluency with the manual alphabet, clocked at 80 words per minute.

By 1890, Helen's fame was steadily growing. American newspapers described her as "the wonder girl" and "the miracle." Stories of her remarkable feats spread around the globe. During that same year, an instructor at Perkins returned from Europe with the exciting news of a Norwegian girl who, like Helen, was blind, deaf, and mute. The girl from Norway received successful speech remediation and learned to speak. When Helen heard about the girl's accomplishment, she told Sullivan, "I must speak."

Boston was also the home of the Horace Mann School, an acclaimed school for the deaf. After meeting Helen, the principal, Sarah Fuller, agreed to offer Helen speech instruction. By having her student feel the position of her tongue and lips as she made various sounds, Fuller taught Helen how to reproduce those sounds. "I was eager to imitate every motion," Helen recalled, "and in an hour had learned six elements of speech: M, P, A, S, T, and I."

Although there was nothing physically wrong with Helen's vocal chords, they were weak and untrained for speech. When after 10 lessons she muttered, "I am not dumb [mute] now," no one except Sullivan and Fuller could comprehend her words. Even though Helen never achieved natural pitch, volume, and enunciation so that others could understand her clearly, she learned from Fuller how to lip-read by touching the lips and throats of people speaking to her.

The inability to speak clearly was a bitter disappointment to Helen, but her optimistic spirit was undaunted. All those who came in contact with her were immediately struck by her warm and generous nature. When the 10-year-old Helen learned of a blind and deaf 5-year-old named Tommy Stringer, who had been placed in a poorhouse in Pennsylvania, she immediately launched a campaign to bring the child to Boston for training at Perkins. By writing letters to friends and to newspapers, Helen's campaign raised $1,600 and Tommy was able to attend Perkins.

Helping Tommy was only the first such benevolent act in Helen's young life. Within a few short years, she and Teacher would be reaching out to other people who needed assistance throughout the world. Helen possessed an un-limited capacity for warmth and kindness. Sullivan's fears that too much publicity would spoil her young student proved to be unfounded. Instead, Helen instinctively chan-neled such attention into unprecedented success in helping others. "I know she is destined to be the instrument of great good in the world," wrote Sullivan, "showing how much can be achieved under the worst difficulties and how sweet life can be under the darkest cloud."

No one was more pleased with Helen's achievements than Perkins's director, Michael Anagnos. Proud of the accomplishments of Anne Sullivan and of her renowned student, Anagnos devoted 200 pages of Perkins's 1891 annual report to the 11-year-old Helen. Despite her young age, Helen realized that Anagnos had been the one who had handpicked Sullivan as her teacher. Since 1886, Anag-nos had demonstrated a profound interest in Helen, and she deeply appreciated his kindness.

On the occasion of his birthday in November 1891, Helen sent Anagnos a special present, describing it as "a little story which I wrote for your birthday gift." Pleased with Helen's story, called "The Frost King," Anagnos had the imaginative fairy tale published. Soon reports circu-lated that Helen's story was not an original tale but bore remarkable similarities to another story, "Frost Fairies," a chapter in Margaret Canby's *Birdie and His Friends,* which was published in 1873. Deeply embarrassed by the allegations that Helen would have deliberately cop-ied the story, Anagnos arranged for a "trial" to take place at Perkins. During the proceedings, eight school repre-sentatives questioned Helen for two hours about the incident.

Helen was completely baffled by the events and al-though she readily admitted that her story was very similar to the previous work, she could not imagine how she could have reproduced the tale. Finally, she concluded that the other story must have been read to her so long ago that "long after I had forgotten it, it came back to me so naturally that I never suspected that it was the child of another mind." With Sullivan's help, the pair eventually determined that the original story had appeared in a book found at the Cape Cod house they had visited three years before. The 11-year-old child had simply forgotten the original version and believed she was creating her own story.

After listening to the testimony, the eight school representatives voted on the charge of plagiarism (stealing the work of another and passing it off as one's own). Had Helen knowingly copied the story? When the votes were cast, there was a tie. Four representatives believed Helen had inadvertently reproduced the story, whereas four others believed Helen was guilty of plagiarism. Anagnos cast the deciding vote of "not guilty," but in a strange turn of events he later changed his original vote to "guilty." With this strong and puzzling act, Anagnos broke off his relationships with both Sullivan and Helen and never again alluded to their names in his annual reports.

No one could understand his motivation for taking these extreme measures with so young a child over such a trivial event. Margaret Canby, the author of the original story, wrote a letter in support of Helen to Anagnos:

> If she had remembered and written down accurately a short story, and that soon after hearing it, it would have been a marvel; but to have heard the story once, three years ago, and in such a way . . . and then to reproduce it so vividly, even adding some touches of her own in perfect keeping with the rest, which really improve the original, is something very few girls of riper years and with every advantage of sight and hearing could have done. Under these circumstances I do not see how anyone can be so unkind as to call it plagiarism.

When the author Mark Twain learned of the incident, he expressed outrage: "Oh, dear me, how unspeakably funny and owlishly idiotic and grotesque was that 'plagia-

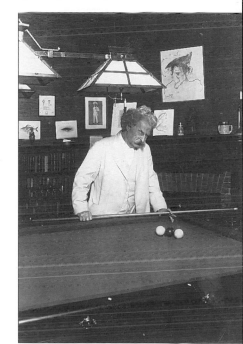

Author Mark Twain, seen here at his home playing billiards, was infuriated by the plagiarism trial that Michael Anagnos conducted against 11-year old Helen. Twain called the incident "owlishly idiotic and grotesque" and said the judges were "a collection of decayed turnips."

Helen and her younger sister, Mildred (right), were very close friends, and in one of her early letters she wrote that she and Mildred "have happy times together." After the plagiarism trial, Helen was apprehensive about writing, even to her friends.

rism' farce!" He added, "To think of those solemn donkeys breaking a little girl's heart with their ignorant damned rubbish." Twain called the judges "a collection of decayed human turnips . . . a gang of dull and hoary pirates piously setting themselves the task of disciplining and purifying a kitten that they think they've caught filching a chop."

The plagiarism incident devastated Helen. "As I lay in my bed that night [after the trial], I wept as I hope few children have wept," Helen later wrote. "I felt so cold, I imagined I should die before morning. . . . I think if this sorrow had come to me when I was older, it would have broken my spirit beyond repairing." Struggling to make sense of her misfortune, Helen approached the charge with a philosophical view, admitting that "this sad experience may have done me some good and set me thinking on some problems of composition." However, she felt profound sorrow over the loss of Anagnos's friendship, writing, "My only regret is that it resulted in the loss of one of my dearest friends, Mr. Anagnos."

Helen remained deeply scarred by the experience and later confessed, "No child ever drank deeper of the cup of bitterness than I did." In her first autobiography, *The Story of My Life,* published in 1903, she wrote, "I have never played with words again for mere pleasure of the game. Indeed, I have ever since been tortured by the fear that what I write is not my own."

Helen and Sullivan returned to Alabama following the plagiarism trial. No sooner had they resettled in Tuscumbia than the editor of *The Youth's Companion* asked Helen to submit an autobiographical article to the popular weekly publication. After having been accused of plagiarism, Helen felt terrorized by the thought of writing and was even reluctant to write to her friends. In spite of this, Sullivan urged her to accept the assignment, hoping Helen would regain her confidence. The article, "My Story," was published with the accompanying introductory note: "Written wholly without help of any sort by a deaf and blind girl, 12 years old, and printed without change." The article received much praise and the magazine paid Helen $100, money that was badly needed in the Keller household.

By 1893, Arthur Keller's financial status had declined as a result of some poor business decisions. He could no longer adequately support his family. Not only did he have to stop paying Sullivan a salary but he began borrowing money from her. When Alexander Graham Bell learned of the Kellers' financial plight, he intervened by funding a trip around the United States for Helen and Sullivan. Bell felt Helen's education would be greatly enhanced if she could actually experience places and things instead of merely reading about them.

First Helen and Sullivan visited Washington, D.C., where, as Bell's guests, they attended President Grover

Helen is seen here reading braille in 1897. Helen's autobiographical article, "My Story," written for The Youth's Companion, *received much acclaim by subscribers, and the $100 fee she earned for the piece helped the Keller household at a time when it needed additional financial support.*

The German exhibition in the Manufacturer's and Liberal Arts Building at the 1893 World's Columbian Exposition, held in Chicago, Illinois, included elaborate iron gates. Helen and Sullivan spent three weeks with Bell at the Exposition, where she touched statues, diamonds, a Viking ship, toys, and anything else she could run her fingers over—with the exception of the Egyptian mummies.

Cleveland's second inauguration and visited the Washington Zoo. Later that spring, Bell accompanied Helen, Sullivan, and Mrs. Keller to Niagara Falls, where Helen delighted in nature's magnificent work. "It is difficult to describe my emotions," she wrote, "when I stood on the point which overhangs the American Falls and felt the air vibrate and the earth tremble. . . . One feels helpless and overwhelmed in the presence of such a force. I suppose you feel so, too, when you gaze up to the stars in the stillness of the night, do you not?"

Following Helen's thirteenth birthday in the summer of 1893, Helen and Sullivan spent three weeks at the World's Columbian Exposition in Chicago, Illinois. Held to honor Columbus's discovery of the New World 400 years earlier, the gigantic fair celebrated America's technological progress since 1492. Helen was allowed to touch every exhibit and she recalled, "I took in the glories of the fair with my fingertips." Helen reveled in her introduction to such objects as uncut diamonds and sculpture from various countries such as India and Egypt that she and Sullivan had read about, although Helen declined to touch the Egyptian mummies. Helen's joy at experiencing so many wonders

caused Sullivan to feel ashamed of the limited scope of
Helen's prior instruction. When she confessed these feelings to Bell, their distinguished benefactor replied, "You
were at least not hampered by preconceived notions, and
I think that an advantage. You did not take to your task
standardized ideas, and your own individuality was so
ingrained that you didn't try to repress Helen's. You must
not lay too much stress on what you were not taught by
others. What we learn from others is of less value than what
we teach ourselves!"

In the summer of 1894, Bell arranged for Anne Sullivan
to address a meeting of the American Association to Promote the Teaching of Speech to the Deaf in Chautauqua,
New York. Helen accompanied her teacher and there they
met John D. Wright and Thomas Humason. These educa-
tors were about to open a school for the deaf in New York
City and they expressed the conviction that they could
teach Helen to speak.

Sullivan's desire for Helen's independence deepened as
the teacher understood the state of Arthur Keller's finances. She knew that Helen would have to support herself
and that speaking would greatly augment her ability to
communicate with others. Gradually, she gently related
her concerns to Helen about her financial instability, but
Helen believed that getting an education would automat-
ically provide an income. "I will devour every book I can
find!" she asserted.

"That is a good way to get educated," replied Sullivan,
"but it is not enough. If you grow up to be a bookworm,
what use will you be to the world? You must think of
something more. . . . But remember no matter what happens, that the real independence you can attain is in your
spirit and mind."

Once again, Alexander Graham Bell intervened by ask-
ing a Boston philanthropist, John Spaulding, to underwrite
Helen's tuition at the Wright-Humason Oral School for the
Deaf in New York City. In October 1894, Helen entered

the new institution with Sullivan at her side. Under Dr. Thomas Humason's instruction, Helen immediately began doing "vocalizing exercises" to teach her to control her voice and achieve a normal pitch, making her voice easier to understand.

The most difficult aspect of Helen's training was lipreading. Although Helen had easily learned to lip-read single words, connected speech or phrases became an arduous task and Helen struggled to master the skill. In addition to the voice exercises and lipreading, Helen studied French, German, geography, and arithmetic. She excelled in academics, but her lipreading efforts remained a great frustration. "I suppose we aimed too high," wrote Helen.

During Helen's two years at the school, she and Sullivan visited many of New York's landmarks, such as the Statue

After the death of her father in 1896, Helen realized that she needed to earn a living and hoped that by receiving a diploma from Radcliffe College her future would be secure. She and Sullivan began their search for a school that would help prepare Helen for Radcliffe's rigorous entrance examination.

of Liberty and Madison Square Garden. They also met author Mark Twain and a future president of the United States, Woodrow Wilson.

Helen's experiences at Wright-Humason whetted her appetite to further her education. As a child, she had declared that she would go to Harvard, but as a 16-year-old, she set her sights on Radcliffe, Harvard's sister college. No one believed that Helen Keller would be able to succeed at a so-called normal institution of higher learning for women. Keller had taken no college preparatory courses and, furthermore, she had the financial aspects of such a place to consider. Her benefactor, John Spaulding, had died in 1896 and she had no other source of income.

Sullivan was among those who doubted the wisdom of Keller's decision to attend Radcliffe, because she was concerned about her own failing vision and the resulting strain on her eyes from helping Helen to study. She wrote to a friend, "It seems to me I cannot endure the thought of going to another school, and at such times it seems as if I had better let another person take my place." But, as always, the loyal Sullivan remained with Keller.

During the summer of 1896, Arthur Keller suddenly died while Helen and Sullivan were visiting Sophia Hopkins in Massachusetts. Helen felt guilty because she had not been in Tuscumbia at the time. It was the hottest period of the year in Alabama and there was always widespread illness in the region during the height of the summer. Concerned about Helen's health, her mother discouraged her from returning to Alabama.

"My father is dead. He died last Saturday at my home in Tuscumbia and I was not there," she wrote to Alexander Graham Bell. "My own dear loving father!" She confessed that she had not comprehended "how dearly I loved my father until I realized that I had lost him." The news of Arthur Keller's death strengthened Sullivan's ambition to help Helen achieve financial independence.

Keller (left) and Sullivan hold a study session outdoors in one of their favorite places, while Keller's Boston terrier, Phiz, devotedly sits at their feet. Sullivan frequently took her student outdoors to learn about plants, animals, and climate.

5

AIMING HIGH

DURING HELEN KELLER'S two years at the Wright-Humason School, she and Sullivan became friends with a literary critic, Lawrence Hutton, and his wife, Eleanor. Mrs. Hutton vowed to raise the necessary funds to underwrite Keller's college education and pay Sullivan's salary. Keller knew that she would have to attend a preparatory school before she could pass Radcliffe's rigorous entrance exams. The Cambridge School for Young Ladies in Cambridge, Massachusetts, was recommended to her for preliminary studies.

The Cambridge School's principal, Arthur Gilman, was skeptical about Keller's ability to succeed at his institution, but he agreed to meet her before making any decision about whether or not to admit her. After their meeting, however, Gilman described her as "this marvelous girl" and warmly welcomed her to the Cambridge School, where she enrolled in September 1896. Keller began her days at Cambridge with high ideals and wrote, "I find that I have four things to learn in my school life here—and indeed in life—to think clearly without hurry or confusion, to love everybody sincerely, to act in everything with the highest motives, and to trust in God unhesitantly."

Those high ideals were soon put to the test. For the first time in their lives, both Keller and Sullivan were in a school with students who could see and hear. No special provisions were made for them. Since the texts were not printed in braille, Sullivan had to spell every word in Keller's hand. Two months later, Keller expressed her frustrations and concerns in a letter. "It takes me a long time to have every word of them [the texts] spelled into my hand. Not one of the text books which I use is in raised print; so of course my work is harder than it would be if I should read my lessons by myself. But it is harder for Teacher than it is for me, because the strain on her poor eyes is so great, and I cannot help worrying about them. Sometimes it really seems as if the tasks we have set ourselves were more than we can accomplish!"

When braille texts eventually arrived, the stress on Sullivan's failing eyes was eased. Keller acquired a braillewriter, which enabled her to push braille keys to produce words in regular English print for her assignments. Keller's grammar professor, Frau Grote, was the first faculty member to learn the manual alphabet. Soon other faculty members and students were learning the system so that they too could communicate with Keller. Even Mr. Gilman learned the system so that he could teach Keller in his English courses. At the end of her first year, Keller took examinations on June 29, 1897, just two days after her 17th birthday. She passed in every subject, earning honors in English and German.

Keller planned to spend two years at Cambridge, but Gilman began to encourage her to lessen her workload and remain for three years. Gilman expressed concerns about Keller spending too much time on her studies and he blamed Sullivan for pushing her student too hard. Sullivan did not agree with Gilman's assessment of the situation and their conflict quickly escalated.

Gilman then wrote to Kate Keller stating that Sullivan was endangering Helen's health by overworking her. He suggested that her daughter and Sullivan be separated. Shocked and confused by Gilman's news from nearly a thousand miles away, Mrs. Keller telegraphed Gilman, authorizing him to become Keller's legal guardian.

Bewildered by the latest events, Keller could not believe that she and Teacher would be separated. Without delay, Sullivan sent a three-word telegram to Kate Keller: "we need you." When Kate Keller received the message, she immediately left for Boston, where she met with Gilman and promptly removed Keller from the school. "I found Mr. Gilman had made cruel use of the authority

Keller runs her fingers over a relief sculpture to "see" the classical scene depicted. Keller and Sullivan prepared night and day for the upcoming Radcliffe examinations; Arthur Gilman, the Cambridge School's principal, accused Sullivan of pushing Keller too hard in her studies.

I had given him," Kate Keller later wrote. "I certainly never dreamed of Miss Sullivan being forced away from Helen. . . . Helen is in perfect physical condition and if she shows any evidence of nervous prostration or overwork I cannot discover it."

It had been the most painful and frightening episode for Keller and Sullivan since the two had been united on March 3, 1886, and they vowed that no one would ever separate them again. Their goal continued to be Keller's admission to Radcliffe and they dedicated themselves to achieving that end.

After leaving the Cambridge School in 1897, Keller and Teacher stayed with their friends, Mr. and Mrs. Joseph Chamberlin, at Red Farm, the Chamberlins' Wrentham home, located near Boston. Life on the farm with the Chamberlins was like a breath of fresh air after several years of living in schools. Sullivan felt uncomfortable residing in institutions and laughingly admitted, "I never was cut out to be a schoolmarm!" For two years, Keller worked with a tutor, Merton S. Keith, to prepare for Radcliffe's rigorous entrance exams. When she was not

Keller feeds a swan while sitting in a rowboat. After leaving the Cambridge School in 1897, Keller studied with a tutor for two years. When she was not reading, she spent her free time outdoors, swimming and canoeing in the summer and tobogganing in the winter.

studying, she swam and canoed during the summer and glided across the lake on a toboggan in the winter months.

Keller welcomed the outdoor activities after hours of hard work with Mr. Keith. Weekly tutorial sessions lasted three hours. Her tutor never learned the manual alphabet, so Sullivan had to translate every word in Keller's hand. Although Keller excelled in foreign languages, she was especially weak in math and Mr. Keith spent hours helping her with algebra and geometry. Confessing her frustration with these "horrid hobgoblins," Keller said, "I cannot see why it is so very important to know that the lines drawn from the extremities of the base of an isosceles triangle to the middle points of the opposite sides are equal! The knowledge doesn't make life any sweeter does it?"

As June 1899 approached, Keller's sessions with Mr. Keith increased to five days per week and included English, history, literature, French, and Latin. Finally, the time arrived for the examinations, and Radcliffe unexpectedly insisted that the tests be read to Keller by a complete stranger to ensure that Keller would receive no extra assistance. Unfortunately, the assigned teacher knew only braille.

Keller had become fluent in the five forms of raised types that were used at the time: New York Point, English Braille, American Braille, Moon Point, and Boston Line embossed letters. She had studied all mathematical work in English Braille. The signs and symbols for American Braille were completely different. Mr. Vining, the test proctor, tried to assist Keller by securing a chart of the American signs, but the chart did not arrive until the day before Keller's test. She stayed up most of that night studying and arrived for the exams exhausted and frustrated.

The Radcliffe examinations were grueling. They contained such questions as, "Where are the following: Arbela, Coryere, Dacia, Lade, Rubicon, Trasimene, and with what famous events is each connected?" One portion of

Radcliffe College, founded in 1879 in Cambridge, Massachusetts, is Harvard College's sister school. This photograph, which shows the gymnasium and Fay House at Radcliffe, was taken around 1900, the year Keller became a student.

the English exam said: "Write a paragraph or two on *Silas Marner.* On the coming of Eppie. On the death of Gabriel. Tell the story of *The Merchant of Venice,* showing how many and what stories are interwoven in it." During the math portion of the tests, Keller struggled. She read the problems very slowly and her fingers became stiff and cramped. Finally, the exam ended and Keller felt despondent. Certain that she had failed, the distressed young woman could now only wait to learn her fate. Several days later, the envelope arrived containing the examination results. Keller had made her mark—the certificate of admission had even stated that she "passed with credit in Advanced Latin."

Passing the exams meant that Keller had jumped only the first hurdle of the entrance procedures. She still needed the approval of Radcliffe's academic board. Keller realized that some board members opposed her admission. Even the school's dean, Agnes Irwin, was skeptical about Keller's capacity to succeed at Radcliffe. In a letter to the board, Keller stated, "I realize the obstacles in the way of my receiving a college education are very great—to others they may seem insurmountable; but dear sir, a true soldier does not acknowledge defeat before the battle."

As Keller waited to learn her fate, she received scholarship offers from Cornell University and the University of Chicago, but her heart was still set on Harvard's sister school. She confessed to a friend, "If I went to any other college it would be thought that I did not pass my examinations for Radcliffe." However, Keller did not have to settle for less than her dreams; when the names of incoming Radcliffe freshmen were published, the name of Helen Adams Keller was listed among them. Four years later, President Woodrow Wilson asked Keller why she had chosen Radcliffe. "Because," she replied, "they didn't want me at Radcliffe and, being stubborn by nature, I chose to override their objections."

Sullivan reads a text and translates the words into Keller's hand while Phiz, a gift to Keller from her Radcliffe classmates, lies at Keller's feet. Sullivan spent at least five hours per day reading to Keller, a routine that strained her already fragile eyesight.

The 20-year-old Keller entered Radcliffe in the fall of 1900. There, she and Sullivan experienced many of the same difficulties they had encountered at the Cambridge School because few materials were available in braille. Day after day, Sullivan sat by Keller's side in the classroom, interpreting into her student's hand everything the lecturer said. Keller wrote to her sister, Mildred, explaining that because her hands were always busy listening, she could not take notes. Instead, she rushed out of each lecture, returned home, and as soon as possible jotted down what she could remember.

Keller also realized that the hours Sullivan spent reading to her were taking an ever worsening toll on Sullivan's already weak eyes. It was common for Sullivan to read to Keller for five or more hours a day and Sullivan later confessed to her ophthalmologist, Dr. Morgan, that it was necessary for her to hold the books so close that they almost touched her eyes.

Dr. Morgan was horrified and cautioned Sullivan against risking permanent blindness, saying, "Your health is more important than Helen Keller's education." After

A confident Keller moves her queen to check Sullivan's chessman during a game of chess at Radcliffe. Keller learned how to play chess at Radcliffe and once complained that she rarely had leisure time, saying "in college there is not time to commune with one's thoughts."

Helen Keller, No.

seeing Dr. Morgan, Sullivan resorted to asking Keller if she wanted certain passages reread. "I lied and declared that I could recall them," Keller later admitted. "As a matter of fact they had slipped from my mind."

Despite her youth, Keller realized the importance of reflection and the time to think about what one was learning, but at Radcliffe she lamented, "I used to have time to think, to reflect, my mind and I. We used to sit together of an evening and listen to the inner melodies of the spirit which one hears only in leisure moments. . . . But in college there is not time to commune with one's thoughts."

At the end of each long day, Keller and Teacher returned to 14 Coolidge Avenue in Cambridge, where they lived in

Keller listens to music by feeling the vibrations of the piano keys and strings. Keller was able to take part in numerous activities with her classmates, and Sullivan often served as her interpreter.

a portion of what had once been a lovely mansion. Keller never felt the same acceptance among Radcliffe's faculty that she had experienced at the Cambridge School. Only Dr. William Nielson, Keller's German professor, learned the manual alphabet. And although Keller's classmates selected her as vice president of her class, only one student, Bertha Beckstroth, learned to write braille. Keller loved poetry and Bertha copied Elizabeth Barrett Browning's *Sonnets from the Portuguese* for her friend. Keller's classmates also presented her with the gift of a Boston terrier named Phiz, the first of many canine companions that Keller, a great dog lover, would own.

With Sullivan acting as interpreter, Keller was able to join in many activities with her classmates. While popping corn and eating éclairs around a fire, the girls held "hen sessions," where they talked about issues of the day affecting life on campus and the world beyond as well. "We stripped everything to the naked skeleton," said Keller. "We were passionately independent."

Although Keller had always loved to write, the painful incident at Perkins had left its scar on her. Still, at Radcliffe, Professor Charles Townsend Copeland did more than anyone to nurture Keller's talents in this area. "When I came to your class last October 1, I was trying with all my might to be like everybody else, to forget as entirely as possible my limitation's peculiar environment," Keller wrote to Copeland. "Now, however, I see the folly of attempting to hitch one's wagon to a star with a harness that does not belong to it. . . ."

In 1902, with Copeland's encouragement, Keller accepted an assignment to write the story of her life for *The Ladies' Home Journal.* The publication would pay Keller $3,000 for the work, money that she and Sullivan badly needed. John Macy, a young Harvard instructor, agreed to edit Keller's work. With Sullivan's help, Keller and Macy made great progress on the project and *The Ladies' Home Journal* published the first installment of "The Story of

My Life" in their April 1902 issue. Four more installments were published.

In 1903, her manuscript was expanded into a book, published by Doubleday, and consisted of three parts: an autobiography, selected letters, and Macy's account of Keller's education, with letters and comments by Sullivan. The book received wide critical acclaim and was eventually printed in 50 languages. "I am charmed with your book—enchanted," wrote her friend Mark Twain. "You are a wonderful creature, the most wonderful in the world—you and your other half together—Miss Sullivan, I mean, for it took the two of you to make and complete a perfect whole." The *New York Sun* published an engrossing, insightful review that also paid homage to Sullivan: "It is perhaps worth reminding the readers that the wonderful feat of dragging Helen Keller out of her hopeless darkness was only accomplished by sacrificing for it another woman's whole life, and if ever the attempt is made in another similar case, it must be made at the same cost."

Although 96 women graduated from Radcliffe in the class of 1904, 97 women crossed the stage to receive their diplomas, for Keller and Teacher walked hand in hand to receive Keller's diploma to the thunderous applause of the audience.

Using funds from the sale of *The Story of My Life,* the 24-year-old Keller and the 38-year-old Sullivan had purchased an old farmhouse in Wrentham, Massachusetts, just before Helen's graduation. The two women set up residence in the house, which was situated on seven neglected acres, and although there were many uncertainties about the path Keller's life would take, she knew her mission. "I shall devote my life to those who suffer from loss of sight," she vowed. She wondered if she should pursue a writing career and sought Sullivan's guidance. "I am your mother in heart and mind," replied Sullivan, "but I do not own you."

At the age of 23, a dignified Keller wears the cap and gown of a college graduate in 1904. Keller and Sullivan walked hand in hand across the stage to receive Keller's Radcliffe diploma to the reverberating ovation of the audience.

Keller investigates the blossoms of a tree on the grounds of her Wrentham, Massachusetts, home. John Macy, who was hired to edit Keller's first autobiography, stretched wires around the yard of her home so Keller could take nature walks without being afraid of wandering off the grounds.

6

HELPING OTHERS

KELLER AND SULLIVAN settled in their new Wrentham home after
Helen's graduation from Radcliffe in June 1904. As Keller's thoughts
poured out, she wrote passionately in her study, which was converted
from a dairy room and two pantries. There she wrote one article after
another about blindness, addressing topics such as education for the
blind, the unique challenges presented to the sightless, and the preven-
tion of blindness. John Macy, who was an editor of *The Youth's
Companion* magazine, continued to act as Keller's editor. He spent a
great deal of time with her, playing checkers and talking about his
views on a myriad of issues, including poverty and labor strikes.
Macy stretched wires around the grounds of the house so Keller could
take walks without fear of straying off her property, and he enter-
tained her with unusual activities that Keller found interesting, such
as reading "nature's braille," the moss-covered letters of tombstones
in cemeteries.

Macy's assistance with Keller's writing lessened the severe strain on Sullivan's eyes. The more closely Sullivan and John Macy worked together, the more intimate they became. Until now, Sullivan's entire life had been devoted to her work and her friendship with Keller, but she and Macy, who was 11 years younger than Sullivan, fell in love. They were married in 1905. The Macys set up residence with Keller in Wrentham and the three continued to work together.

In 1908, Keller's next book, *The World I Live In,* was published. A collection of essays in which Keller explained how she used her sense of smell and vibrations to compensate for the loss of her vision and hearing, it received praise from reviewers. But Keller, growing weary of writing solely about herself, later explained, "I found myself utterly confined to one subject—myself, and it was not long before I exhausted it." Her friendship with Macy had deepened her interests in social causes and Keller turned her attentions to the world beyond Wrentham.

Anne Sullivan (far right) leans over the shoulder of her husband, John Macy, while Keller talks to him using the manual alphabet. Macy, who married Sullivan in 1905, encouraged Keller's interests in social causes, such as labor reform and women's suffrage.

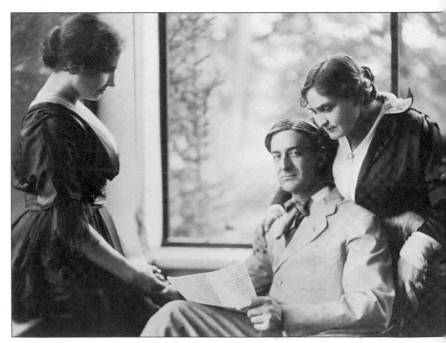

America stood on the threshold of important social reforms in 1909, including women's suffrage, labor reforms, and the prohibition of alcohol. From a global perspective, disarmament became an issue as conflicts mounted between several European countries.

Focusing her attention on women's rights, Keller became engrossed in helping women attain the right to vote. In addition to women's suffrage, Keller was interested in educating the public about the venereal disease gonorrhea, which caused infants to be born blind. Babies born to infected women were in danger of picking up the bacterium that causes gonorrhea during birth. These infants could develop the disease in their eyes, resulting in blindness. Today, most states require that the eyes of newborn babies be treated with drops of silver nitrate or an antibiotic solution to prevent blindness from gonorrhea, but in 1913 such preventative practices were not mandated and few people dared to mention the subject in public. Many Americans who saw Keller as the grown version of the little blind, deaf, and mute girl whom they had come to

In 1913, women march in Washington, D.C., demanding a constitutional amendment that would give them the right to vote. Keller marched in a "Votes for Women" parade and was an ardent supporter of the women's suffrage movement, which attained its goal in 1920.

Scottish-born American industrialist and philanthropist Andrew Carnegie offered to pay Keller an annual pension to help solve her financial problems. Keller, however, initially refused his generous proposition, saying, "I already have a fair share and millions have less than their rightful portion."

adore expressed shock that she would discuss gonorrhea. Furthermore, they had little interest in her views on women's suffrage, preferring instead that she discuss only her physical conditions or her own accomplishments.

Keller's new social consciousness also reshaped her thinking on accepting benevolent financial gifts. The money that she earned from writing was not enough to support herself adequately, yet when the American industrialist Andrew Carnegie offered Keller an annual pension, she refused, saying, "I already have a fair share and millions have less than their rightful portion."

The enthusiasm Keller possessed about social causes renewed her interest in public speaking. With the help of Charles White, a voice teacher from the Boston Conservatory of Music, Keller resumed her attempts to learn to speak. White taught Keller at her Wrentham home each weekend for three years, never charging a fee for his work. Arriving each Saturday, White, who learned the manual alphabet in order to communicate with Keller, stayed until Sunday. Instructing her to sing an octave, he would strike a tuning fork (a two-pronged metal instrument that gives a fixed tone when struck) to measure Helen's pitch. Keller's voice gradually became much more pleasing to listeners and she was optimistic about speaking before audiences.

In addition to speaking and the manual alphabet, Helen had become quite adept at reading lips by vibration. By placing the middle finger on the speaker's nose, her forefinger on the lips, and her thumb on the larynx, she could "hear" what people were saying.

In 1913, Keller's third book was published. *Out of the Dark,* a collection of essays on Keller's social views, was not well received. Keller had counted on profits from the book to bolster her empty bank account. As Helen's financial situation worsened, other tensions surfaced within the Wrentham household. John Macy had always been a heavy drinker, and his alcohol habit intensified, causing marital problems that deeply distressed Sullivan. In addition, the years of service to Keller had taken their toll on Sullivan, leaving her exhausted and her eyes severely damaged. She had also gained a great deal of weight, further complicating her health problems.

By 1913, the stress over finances and Sullivan's failing marriage mounted. John Macy's alcoholism and his extravagant tastes in clothing, books, and travel further eroded the little money that Keller and Teacher had to live on. In a letter to her sister, Keller later wrote, "From the year 1905, when Teacher was married, until 1920, when

Keller reads the lips of a child by placing her forefinger on the girl's lips and her thumb on the child's larynx. In addition to becoming quite proficient in lipreading, Keller worked to improve her own voice so that she could speak before audiences and be understood.

I rose up in my wrath and said John should not have another penny of my earnings, we were constantly paying considerable sums for him—for his family, for his tailors, his books, and a trip of four months and a half in Europe, and for any one he wished to assist. . . ."

Keller and Sullivan knew that they had no time to wring their hands in despair. They needed income and Keller decided to try out her new speaking skills before audiences. Both women realized that a lecture tour was a risky venture, for Sullivan was in no condition to travel and audiences might not be able to clearly understand Keller's voice. But they urgently needed the money, so the two women apprehensively embarked on a speaking tour throughout the United States.

In 1913, Keller made her first appearance in Montclair, New Jersey. Before Keller spoke, her longtime friend, Alexander Graham Bell, introduced her to the crowd. "Terror invaded my flesh, I felt my voice soaring, and I knew that meant falsetto," she later wrote. "Frantically I dragged it down till my words fell about me like bricks." When her speech ended, she walked off the stage and dissolved in tears of humiliation and frustration. However, through the floorboards of the stage's wings, she suddenly felt a great vibration and she instantly recognized the trembling as applause. The audience had loved listening to her and they wildly applauded for what seemed like an eternity to Keller and Sullivan. Afterward, Bell said to Keller, "You have learned to speak, and I believe you are meant to break down the barriers which separate the deaf from mankind. . . . There are unique tasks waiting for you, a unique woman."

Audiences could not clearly comprehend all of her words, so Keller and Sullivan found ways to improve Keller's presentation. Before introducing her well-known student, Sullivan opened each lecture with a brief talk about the methods that she had used to teach her student. They demonstrated lipreading, and finally, Keller spoke

After John Macy's unfortunate drain on the money of the Wrentham household and his and Anne's marital separation, Keller and Sullivan forged ahead with their plans for a lecture tour. Although they realized it would be a gamble, they needed funds desperately and were willing to give public speaking a try.

to the audience. Her appearances turned out to be more successful than she had originally imagined they would be.

While Keller and Sullivan toured the country in 1914, John Macy moved out of the Wrentham home. Although the marriage had ended, the Macys never legally divorced and Keller and Sullivan maintained contact with John until his death in 1932.

During a lecture appearance in Maine, Sullivan suddenly became very ill with the flu. When she later collapsed in the hotel room, Keller was terrified because she could not use the telephone or find her way out of the room. Although many blind people possess a special ability to navigate well in strange places, Keller never had such an ability, and she was totally helpless in new surroundings. She later confessed, "My helplessness terrified me." The two women remained alone in the room until Teacher was able to telephone for a doctor. With the help of the hotel

While on the lecture circuit, Sullivan, Keller, and a friend discuss ways in which they can improve their presentation. Sullivan usually opened each lecture by discussing her methods of teaching Keller. She would then introduce her student, and Keller and she would demonstrate lipreading before Keller actually spoke to the crowd.

staff, Keller and Sullivan boarded a train and returned home.

During the short train trip to Massachusetts, Keller was struck by the gravity of the situation. The crisis in Maine caused her to realize that her beloved Teacher could not cope with the demands placed on her. She knew that they needed help, someone to assist them as a secretary and companion if they were to continue on the lecture circuit.

Arriving at Wrentham, Keller immediately wrote to Andrew Carnegie, her would-be benefactor, telling him that she had been foolish to refuse his earlier offer of financial assistance. Carnegie quickly sent a check and a letter expressing his admiration for Keller. He wrote, "There are a few great souls who can rise to the height of allowing others to do for them what they would like to do for others. . . . And so you have risen. I am happy indeed—one likes to have his words of wisdom appreciated. Remember, Mrs. Carnegie and I are the two to be thankful, for it is beyond question more blessed to give than receive."

Polly Thomson, a young Scotswoman, was hired to assist Keller and Sullivan. Although Thomson had never heard of Keller and did not know the manual alphabet, she quickly proved to be a great asset. In addition to managing the household, the young woman, who was six years younger than Keller, served as a secretary, maintaining the finances, planning schedules for upcoming lecture tours, and mapping out travel routes. She styled hair and manicured nails, and could even cook in a pinch. In 1914, the three women set out on Keller's next lecture tour, and Thomson's competent presence became invaluable to her companions.

When World War I ignited in Europe in 1914, Keller took a neutral stance on the fighting. Her study of German in college had cultivated an interest in and fondness for the German culture. When she was accused of harboring German sympathies, she responded, "I am neutral, yes, but I consider my second country the land of Beethoven, Goethe, Kant, and Karl Marx." As she toured the New England states in the fall, she came to dread questions from audiences about her views on the war. When asked if she was neutral, Keller was glad to answer "yes," also adding, "I liked the people of all nations, but not their armies and navies." The 34-year-old Keller became an adept speaker and even learned to handle hecklers with her quick wit. When a man once shouted, "Which part of the brain do you use?" Keller shot back, "The whole of it. What part do you use?"

The three women continued to tour through much of the next two years until Sullivan became ill in 1916. Fearing that she had tuberculosis, a contagious disease that primarily affects the lungs, doctors recommended that Sullivan stay in a sanitarium in Saranac, New York. Thomson would accompany Sullivan and Kate Keller came from Alabama to stay with her daughter. Keller and her mother hired a secretary, 29-year-old Peter Fagan, to assist them during a summer lecture tour. Fagan, a journalist who had taught himself braille and who knew the manual alphabet, immediately struck up a friendship with Keller. The two got along well and shared common views on the war and social issues. Conversely, Kate Keller did not share their political views and she developed a strong dislike for the young man.

The thought of being separated from Sullivan had thrown Keller into a tailspin of isolation and confusion. Fagan's presence had coincided with a bleak time in her life. Uncertain if Teacher would ever be able to return to her, Keller felt lost and wondered how she could continue her work. It was obvious to everyone that Keller and Fagan were falling in love with each other and it was an entirely new experience for Keller, who had never imagined herself romantically involved with anyone. Recalling those tumultuous days, Keller later wrote, "His love was a bright sun that shone upon my helplessness and isolation. The

Keller and Sullivan are photographed on a railroad platform in 1913. After Sullivan's collapse in Maine, it was clear that she could no longer handle the demands placed on her, and Keller decided the time had come to hire someone to assist them.

sweetness of being loved enchanted me, and I yielded to an imperious longing to be part of a man's life."

Kate Keller, however, remained violently opposed to the young couple's relationship. She might have feared that Fagan would quickly grow weary of caring for Helen and break her heart by leaving her. Mrs. Keller might also have been concerned about her daughter wanting but not being able to raise a child. Whatever her motivations, Mrs. Keller was determined to end the relationship. Consequently, Helen said nothing to her mother about her romantic ties with Fagan, although she longed to tell the world of her happiness. When Fagan proposed to Keller, she gladly accepted and the two devised a plan to secretly elope.

A few days later, Keller stood in her bedroom brushing her hair when Kate Keller burst into the room, clutching a newspaper in her hand. Shaking with rage, her fingers quivered as she spelled a message in her daughter's hand. The *Boston Globe* ran a story reporting that Keller and Fagan had applied for a marriage license at Boston's city hall.

Mrs. Keller was enraged by her daughter's hidden intentions. "What have you been doing with that creature?" she asked Keller. "The papers are full of a dreadful story about you and him. What does it all mean?" she inquired.

Although the 36-year-old Keller had never been filled with such terror, outwardly she remained calm. Continuing to slowly brush her hair, she flatly denied any knowledge of the matter and claimed that the newspaper had made a mistake. Sullivan, who was confined to her bed, was to leave the following day for Saranac. Both Sullivan and Mrs. Keller were convinced that Keller would tell Teacher the truth, and Keller's mother dragged her daughter to Sullivan's bedside. But Keller continued to deny the allegations. "My mother ordered the young man out of the house that very day," Keller later wrote. "She would not even let him speak to me, but he wrote me a note in Braille, telling me where he would be, and begging me to keep him informed."

During the next several days, the newspapers were filled with reports denying the marriage license application. One report issued by Fagan claimed that he was, indeed, engaged to another young woman, although he refused to give her name. However, no one could deny the fact that the city registrar showed that the license application had been made jointly by Keller and Fagan; their signatures attested to that truth.

Kate Keller decided to take action and return with her daughter to Tuscumbia. She booked passage on a boat to Savannah, Georgia, where they would take the train on to Montgomery. But after learning that Fagan planned to be aboard to meet Helen, Mrs. Keller suddenly changed their plans and traveled to Alabama by train. Fagan, meanwhile, made the boat trip alone.

When they arrived at Ivy Green, Mrs. Keller felt enormously relieved that the ordeal was over. But she was mistaken about seeing the last of Fagan. One day, while she was upstairs, her daughter Mildred rushed up to report that a young man was on the front porch with Keller, spelling words in her hand. Mildred's husband, Warren Tyson, was quickly summoned, and Fagan suddenly found himself staring down the barrel of a rifle. He was not one to give up, however, and vowed to return for Keller.

Several nights later, Mildred was awakened by a sound outside. Investigating, she and her husband discovered Helen on the front porch. Somehow, Fagan had gotten word to Keller that he would come for her, and she anxiously waited on the porch all night. But Fagan, apparently frightened by the threat of the rifle-bearing Tyson, never came that night and Keller and Fagan never encountered each other again.

Ten years after what she described as the most painful event of her life, Keller wrote, "I seem to have acted exactly opposite to my nature. It can be explained only in

Keller waters a plant on the porch of her home. Peter Fagan's friendship during Sullivan's recuperation from tuberculosis boosted Keller's confidence during a very lonely period in her life. Of her romance with Fagan, Keller later wrote, "His love was a bright sun that shone upon my helplessness and isolation."

the old way—that love makes us blind and leaves the mind confused and deprives it of the use of judgment. I corresponded with the young man for several months; but my love dream was shattered. It had flowered under an inauspicious star. The unhappiness I had caused my dear ones produced a state of mind unfavorable to the continuance of my relations with the young man. The love which had come unseen and unexpected departed with tempest on its wings."

But perhaps Keller best expressed her sadness in a poem she wrote around 1917:

> What earthly consolation is there for one like me
> Whom fate has denied a husband and the joy of
>   motherhood?
> At the moment my loneliness seems a void that will
>   always be immense.
> Fortunately I have much to do.
> More than ever before, in fact,
> And while doing it, I shall have confidence as always,
> That my unfilled longings will be gloriously satisfied
> In a world where eyes never grow dim, nor ears dull.

Keller began to think of her future, of the work she had to do. Above all, she prayed for Teacher's recovery so that they could be reunited.

Dressed in her riding habit, Keller goes for an outing in the countryside in 1919. Keller had first taken riding lessons when she attended the Wright-Humason School, and she was always enthusiastic about participating in such activities.

7

COMBINING
WORK AND FAME

AFTER ANNE SULLIVAN'S RECOVERY from tuberculosis, Keller and Sullivan were reunited in 1917. The United States entered World War I that year, and audiences were in no mood to hear about Keller's antiwar views. Revenues from lecture tours dropped sharply. To save money, the two women sold their Wrentham home and moved into a smaller house in Forest Hills, a neighborhood in Queens, which is a borough of New York City. But financial problems continued to plague them.

Silent movies were a popular medium of entertainment and Hollywood recognized that the story of Keller and Sullivan would make a fascinating film. In 1918, Keller, Sullivan, and Thomson set out for California where they met with two great film stars, Mary Pickford and Douglas Fairbanks, Sr. Their idea was for Helen to make a movie to benefit the blind. Even the popular actor Charlie Chaplin volunteered to appear in the film.

In 1918, in Hollywood, California, Polly Thomson (seated at left), Helen Keller (center), and Anne Sullivan (right) watch the filming of Deliverance, *a silent picture based on the story of Keller's life, while comedian Charlie Chaplin explains the scene.*

Talking moving pictures, or "talkies," had not yet been invented; movies were still black-and-white silent productions, in which the actors' voices could not be heard. Instead, the dialogue appeared on the screen while a pianist played background music. Silent films were a perfect medium for Keller. She recognized their power for focusing America's attention on the special needs of the blind. In addition, Keller had been told that she might earn a salary in the range of $50,000 to $100,000 if she would agree to make the movie.

Keller and Sullivan sought to maintain the integrity of the story of Helen's life by keeping the script and the film, which was to be called *Deliverance*, factual. However, as they soon learned, Hollywood did not share their objective. The film's producer and director wanted dramatic scenes and elaborate staging and costumes. "We started out to make an honest picture of my life, my struggles, triumphs, and aspirations," wrote Helen, "but towards that end we seem to have fallen down somehow." It was obvious that *Deliverance* would not accurately portray Keller's life. Released with a massive publicity campaign, the film flopped at the box office and was a financial disaster.

Although Keller and Sullivan received little money from the project, the experience caused them to reconsider Arthur Keller's earlier suggestion, made several years before, that his daughter appear on the vaudeville circuit. Pride had originally prevented Keller from considering such activity. She did not want to appear on the same stage with comedians, magicians, and similar acts. But in 1919, finances, not pride, dictated her decision making and she and Sullivan signed a lucrative contract for a nationwide theatrical tour.

Once again, Keller, Sullivan, and Thomson embarked on a tour of the country, presenting a 20-minute performance in which they related the story of Keller's education. They concluded their presentation by taking questions from the audience. Helen enjoyed the vaudeville circuit, but the rigors of traveling strained the 54-year-old Sullivan's failing health.

The theatrical motto "The show must go on" soon tested Keller's true mettle in July 1921. Two hours before she was to go onstage for a Los Angeles performance, Keller received a telegram from her sister, Mildred, informing her that their mother had suddenly died in Alabama. Heartbroken, Helen still performed that night, laughing and joking with the audience like the trouper she had become. Because Keller had signed contracts to perform through April 1922, she could not even go home to attend her mother's funeral. When Sullivan became ill in January, Thomson filled in as a substitute during the remainder of the tour. The author Carl Sandburg saw Keller perform in Chicago and wrote to her afterward: "Possibly the finest thing about your performance is that those who hear and see you feel that zest for living, the zest you radiate, is more important than any formula about how to live life."

In 1919, Keller and Sullivan joined the vaudeville circuit, presenting the details of Keller's education to audiences around the country. The ordeal of traveling, however, soon took its toll on Sullivan's declining health.

Finally, the tour ended and Keller could visit her sister in Tuscumbia. There, she felt as if she was experiencing her mother's death for the second time and she longed to return to her New York home. She invited Mildred and her three daughters to come to Queens with her in June. Sullivan was weary from the ordeal of touring, and Keller and Thomson joined her for a long respite.

By 1924, Keller had exhausted her appeal on the vaudeville circuit, and she and Sullivan began to think about another means of earning income. When Thomson returned to Scotland during the summer to visit her family, Keller and Sullivan decided to make plans for their future during a camping trip to Maine and Canada. Accompanied by their loyal chauffeur, Harry Lamb, Keller and Sullivan reveled in the solitude and clean air of the countryside, far from New York's fast-paced lifestyle.

As Keller watched Sullivan's health deteriorate, she was plagued by concern and a sense of guilt that Teacher had sacrificed her vision, her health and, indeed, her life for her student. Keller's worry grew as the effects of travel, fatigue, and eye strain increased. Nevertheless, the two women found a special solace during their outdoor expedition. Lamb helped them pitch tents and chop firewood under the magnificent evergreens. Camping on the banks of the Kennebunk River, Keller and Teacher escaped from the daily visitors, the mail, and the telephone calls that had come to define their lives in New York. Keller later confessed, "I was released for a while from the remorseful thought (she never in her life suggested it) that perhaps her individuality was subordinated to my own."

Before departing on their trip, Sullivan and Keller had talked with the staff of the American Foundation for the Blind about working at fund-raising for the organization. By October 1924, their finances had eroded so much that they sold their car and released their chauffeur.

Later that month, Keller and Sullivan signed a contract to raise $2 million in endowments for the American Foun-

Cowboy humorist Will Rogers, who admired Keller and Sullivan's work, asked on his radio show for donations to the American Foundation for the Blind on Keller's behalf. Keller and Sullivan had agreed to raise $2 million for the foundation.

dation for the Blind during a six-month period. The two women would make four appearances each week for a salary of $2,000 per month. The fund-raising appearances proved to be almost as arduous as the vaudeville circuit. The trio maintained an exhausting schedule. Helen wrote, "For three years we traveled the country from coast to coast. We addressed 250,000 people at 249 meetings in 123 cities."

"Like many crusaders," wrote biographer Joseph P. Lash, "Helen assumed that right had only to be proclaimed and the virtuous would flock to the banner." But Helen soon learned that fund-raising was a very political process. When the Foundation expressed concern about the potential of Keller's political views harming the fund-raising efforts, she agreed to censor her political comments during the campaign. Occasionally, however, Keller yielded to temptation. Once, while sitting next to a governor who was a member of the Ku Klux Klan, she informed him that she was "a Catholic, anti-Klan, and a socialist." Waiting for his reaction, she was surprised when he thrust out his hand and wanted to shake hers. In her autobiographical *Midstream,* published in 1929, she wrote, "We came to understand what must be the exhaustion of campaigning political candidates, but we had an advantage over the politicians: they met divided support while our cause appealed to all parties."

As the Foundation had known all along, Keller's name was magic. Soon, Keller and Sullivan had won generous contributions from oil baron John D. Rockefeller and automobile tycoon Henry Ford. Will Rogers, the popular cowboy humorist, requested donations for Keller's work during his radio broadcasts.

During an appearance at Philadelphia's Academy of Music, Keller's friend, editor Edward Bok, introduced her, exclaiming, "We are often tempted to say, 'What can we do?' We're only one, and how can we do anything? And that with all our faculties! Then look at Helen Keller and see what she has done—blind and deaf as she is—and see if you can ever again ask such a question about yourself." During that single afternoon fund-raiser, they raised $21,000. One newspaper carried the headline: PURSES FLY OPEN TO HELEN KELLER.

By the end of 1924, Keller was struck by the enormity of their obligation to raise such a large quantity of money in such a brief time. She wrote to her sister, Mildred, "Oh my, what a strenuous business this beggar's life. We set out to raise that large sum in six months, and now it seems a thousand years ahead."

Keller's optimistic nature allowed her to view the fund-raising campaign as a challenge, but Sullivan did

In 1926, President Calvin Coolidge welcomes Keller, Sullivan, and Thomson as they open a fund-raising drive for the American Foundation for the Blind in the nation's capital. Unlike Keller, Sullivan was pessimistic about their project with the Foundation and disliked the demeaning aspect of fund-raising

not share Keller's enthusiasm and the rigors of travel compounded her pessimistic attitude toward the entire project. Teacher disliked the groveling aspect of fund-raising. Helen sensed that Sullivan also regretted that she was not able to pursue her own interests. "If Teacher had been left free to choose her destiny," Helen later wrote in *Teacher: Anne Sullivan Macy,* "she would never have limited herself to the cause of the blind. It was only because she saw a chance of usefulness to them that she joined her wealth of mind and heart to my endeavors."

In 1927, unable to reach a satisfactory new agreement with the Foundation, Keller and Sullivan decided to end their affiliation with the organization. Sullivan, a formidable negotiator, had tried to secure a larger salary, but her attempts were unsuccessful. The pair felt that the Foundation was unfairly using Keller's name without adequate compensation. Keller and Sullivan decided to launch another writing project.

When Keller's autobiography, *The Story of My Life,* had been published in 1903 by Doubleday, the publisher had been delighted with the impressive number of sales. In 1927, Doubleday continued to be amazed at how well the book had sold and they were anxious for Keller to write another installment. Keller, however, expressed apprehension about undertaking such a huge project. Without the assistance of an able editor and concerned about Sullivan's failing eyes and health, Keller resisted the idea.

When Doubleday offered to provide Keller with an editorial assistant, Nella Braddy, Keller agreed to take on the project. Soon, though, she decided that she did not wish to write an autobiography and the project turned into a book about her religious beliefs, entitled *My Religion.*

Keller had become a disciple of the teachings of Emanuel Swedenborg, an 18th-century Swedish scientist, inventor, and mystical religious leader. Claiming that his views were based on Bible teachings that had been interpreted to him through direct communications with the

Sullivan, Keller, and Thomson set out on a cruise to southern France with the funds Keller received from her 1927 book, My Religion. *About her spiritual life, Keller wrote, "I cannot imagine myself without religion. I could as easily fancy a living body without a heart. To one who is deaf and blind, the spiritual world offers no difficulty."*

spiritual world, he wrote a number of books detailing his "heavenly doctrines." Swedenborg taught that he had been called to reveal deeper spiritual meanings in Scripture. He placed more importance on the spiritual aspect of life, rather than on the adherence to strict codes of living. His followers were known as Swedenborgians and they established the General Church of the New Jerusalem.

The emphasis Swedenborg placed on the spiritual aspect of existence fit into Keller's life experience. "He did not make a new Bible, but the Bible all new," wrote Keller in *My Religion*. Responding to his claim to have been in touch with another world, she wrote, "That is nothing new to my experience. Daily I place implicit faith in my friends and their eyes and ears, and they tell me how often their senses deceive and lead them astray. Yet out of their evidence I gather countless precious truths with which I build my world, and my soul is enabled to picture the beauty of the sky and listen to the song of birds. All about me is silence and darkness, yet within me, in the spirit, is music and brightness, and colour flashes through all my thoughts."

My Religion was published in 1927 and was well received by the critics and the public alike. Keller best expressed her beliefs on the book's final page: "I cannot imagine myself without religion. I could as easily fancy a living body without a heart. To one who is deaf and blind, the spiritual world offers no difficulty."

With Nella Braddy's assistance, Keller continued working on her next autobiographical account, *Midstream,* which was published in 1929. For the first time, some critics questioned Keller's use of expressive language, wondering how a blind and deaf person could so accurately describe objects and ideas through poetic language such as, "I have the immeasurable fires of the mind for light." "She talks bookishly," wrote Robert M. Coates, an interviewer for *New Yorker* magazine. "Never having heard a voice," he explained, "she had never learned the easy vocabulary of ordinary discourse. To express her ideas, she falls back on the phrases she has learned from books, and uses words that sound stilted, poetical metaphors."

Although the criticism stung Keller, it served to ignite a fascinating and timely examination of the issue of sensory impressions in blind and deaf people among philosophers, physicians, and psychologists. One Scottish otologist (a physician who specializes in the treatment of ear diseases), Dr. James Kerr Love, concluded that children who lose their sight or hearing later in childhood lose language or visual impressions if they do not have a teacher to help them retrieve that information. In Keller's case, Dr. Love believed that before the age of 19 months, Helen had both language and visual impressions that Sullivan helped her to recall. Love wrote, "Those vivid impressions of early childhood—those of colour and sound . . . those impressions for a time lost their names, but the precepts were not lost." He quoted lines from William Wordsworth's poem "Intimations of Immortality from Recollections of Early Childhood":

> There was a time when meadow, grove, and stream,
> The earth and every common sight
> To me did seem
> Apparell'd in celestial light
> The glory and the freshness of a dream.

Keller spoke as she wrote, with a lovely poetic phrasing, in a style that many people who had their eyesight and hearing envied. These talents that Teacher had so long ago recognized in her student were Keller's greatest gifts.

Keller reads a braille text in the library of her Westport, Connecticut, home in 1955. During the 1950s, Keller continued to champion programs for the physically challenged around the world. In exchange for her efforts, she received some of the highest international honors, including France's Legion of Honor and Japan's Sacred Treasure Award.

8

"LIFE, AN EXCITING BUSINESS"

WHEN THE STOCK MARKET CRASHED in late October 1929, the nation faced the greatest economic depression it had ever seen. Factories cut production, construction slowed, and millions of people lost their life's savings in the more than 5,000 banks that failed during the first three years of the crisis. As the catastrophe continued, more than 40 million Americans found themselves out of work. The suffering became overwhelming. Keller's situation, however, improved. In 1930, her finances were bolstered by a trust fund established by her friend Eleanor Hutton.

Keller, Sullivan, and Thomson, who were now dubbed the "Forest Hills Three Musketeers," embarked on their first tour of Europe in 1930. Sullivan's eyesight was failing rapidly and Keller wanted Teacher to see the world, especially the Sullivan family's native Ireland. The women enjoyed their tour and stayed in Europe longer than they had planned. Reflecting on their lives, Keller wrote in her autobiography, "We have spent our days, as it were, in a railroad station, meeting many, but knowing few." Now it was time to slow their pace and savor the world.

While in Europe, Helen celebrated her 50th birthday and her friend and editor, Nella Braddy, reported Helen's words at the time: "It was good not to have to wear a company smile and make a speech about being fifty years young."

The three women returned from Europe in 1932, and Keller renewed her affiliation with the American Foundation for the Blind. However, Sullivan remained at home while Keller and Thomson took to the road. The rigors of fund-raising were too hard on the aging Sullivan.

A major advancement for the blind occurred in 1932 when Louis Braille's system of raised dots was internationally adopted as a standardized system of reading and writing for the blind, replacing the four other systems. This was a great achievement, and one that Keller had campaigned for vigorously. It meant that all materials for the blind would become available in one system that everyone could learn to understand.

During the summer of 1936, the Forest Hills trio rented a cottage on eastern Long Island, escaping the heat of Queens and providing the 70-year-old Sullivan with fresh air and ocean breezes. Although feeble, Sullivan surprised Keller and Thomson one day by walking alone to the beach and joining them at the water's edge. As the three women waded in the surf, Sullivan suddenly collapsed. Keller and Thomson led her back to the house and summoned a doctor, but Sullivan had suffered a stroke and she never recovered from it. Once, during her illness, she told Keller, "I am trying so hard to live for you." Sullivan died on October 20, 1936; Keller was devastated, but she demonstrated amazing strength in facing the loss of her beloved Teacher.

"They were two in one, one in two," said Keller's former publisher, Russell Doubleday, describing the unique relationship of Helen Adams Keller and Anne Sullivan Macy. At the funeral services, a friend, writer Alexander Woollcott, made these notes as Keller and Thomson passed his pew: "I saw the swift, bird-like fluttering of Helen's hands—saw and with a quickened heartbeat knew what I had seen—Helen—think of it – Helen comforting her companion."

Many people speculated after Sullivan's death that Keller would return to Alabama and live with her sister, Mildred. However, with Thomson at her side, she remained in New York and looked forward to carrying on her work for humanity. In 1937, accepting an invitation by Japan's director of the Lighthouse for the Blind (an organization that founded centers throughout the

In September 1937, Keller visits her half brother Simpson in Dallas, Texas, upon her return from the Japan tour. Her dog Kamituze, whose name means "wings of gold," was a gift from the Japanese.

world, where blind people could socialize and have recreation) in Osaka, Keller and Thomson toured Japan, visiting 39 cities. Keller delivered 97 lectures in which she talked to audiences about the needs of the disabled and her dream of world peace. In the ancient city of Nara, Keller touched the great bronze Buddha, a sacred shrine to Buddhists.

Upon her return to the United States, Keller immediately went to work to complete *Journal*. Published in 1938, the account of Helen's life carried great symbolism and concluded with the completion of her tour of Japan. She wanted everyone to realize that, although she had lost Teacher, her life's work would continue. In *Journal's* final entry, which described how Sullivan's spirit continued to live in her and Polly, Keller wrote, "But Polly and I notice that strength flows into us for tasks to which we never dreamed we should be equal."

Keller worked for the American Foundation for the Blind once again, and her efforts took on a new importance. In 1935, the Social Security Act had been passed by Congress, which provided old age pensions and funds for, among others, the disabled, including the blind. These funds purchased braille materials and paid for the production of talking-book records. The American Foundation for the Blind launched a campaign to supply the blind with machines that would play the talking books. Keller initially opposed the talking books because they were not effective for use with those who were deaf. Gradually, however, she changed her mind, realizing that many blind people benefited from the recorded books, and she agreed to raise funds for the project.

Executives of the Foundation knew that Keller had friends in high places and they recognized her potential to win the support of many powerful individuals. Keller immediately elicited the help of her longtime friend Will Rogers, who again agreed to do radio spots for Keller's cause. When Rogers sat next to President Franklin D.

Keller (center) and Thomson visit a farm in Scotland in 1939. Keller called her new home in Westport, Connecticut, Arcan Ridge, after a farmhouse in South Arcan, Scotland. She and Sullivan had visited South Arcan years earlier and Keller wanted to honor Sullivan by naming her new home after one of their happiest memories.

Roosevelt at a dinner for the Democratic party, the popular humorist mentioned his own radio spots on behalf of the blind. Roosevelt, whose legs were paralyzed by poliomyelitis, responded by passing a note to Rogers, "Anything Helen Keller is for, I am for."

In 1938, Keller and Thomson moved into a new home in Westport, Connecticut, a gift from the American Foundation for the Blind. Wanting to name her new home in honor of Anne Sullivan, Keller called it Arcan Ridge, after the farmhouse in South Arcan, Scotland, "where Teacher and I were so happy together." The white colonial-style house with green shutters was surrounded by brooks, woods, meadows, and the traditional New England stone walls. Keller and Thomson planted fragrant flowers that Keller would especially enjoy, including her favorite, lily of the valley. She also had a spacious library with 35 shelves for her massive collection of braille books.

Keller devoted much of her time to writing a biography of Sullivan, something she had been planning to do for many years. After settling into her new home, she compiled notes, diaries, and correspondence. Although she worked diligently on the book about Teacher, Keller would take nearly 20 years to complete it.

When the United States entered World War II in 1941, Keller wanted very much to help in the war effort. Although she had always been a staunch pacifist, Keller was incensed by Japan's attack on the U.S. naval base at Pearl Harbor, Hawaii, on December 7, 1941, and she wished to support the nation's endeavors to win the war. Eventually, Keller found great satisfaction in visiting the wounded

In 1942, Keller moves her sensitive fingers over a bust that the renowned sculptor Jo Davidson (center) has made of her.

soldiers in military hospitals and focused her attentions on those soldiers who were blinded or deafened in battle. Keller initially wondered how the young wounded soldiers would relate to her, a matronly older woman giving them encouragement, but her apprehensions were soon erased by their warm response to her. Despite Keller's status as a celebrity who had led a life filled with enriching experiences traveling around the world and meeting famous dignitaries, she said that visiting the wounded soldiers was "the crowning experience of my life."

After the war ended in 1945, former first lady Eleanor Roosevelt accepted an award from the American Foundation for the Blind for her late husband, President Franklin Roosevelt. Keller presented the award to Mrs. Roosevelt, and after listening to Keller speak, Mrs. Roosevelt said, "As I stood and listened to Miss Keller speak, I thought how wonderfully both Miss Keller and my husband typified the triumph over physical handicap."

In 1946, Helen and Thomson went on a tour of Europe for the American Foundation for the Overseas Blind. While in Rome, Keller and Thomson received the news that their home, Arcan Ridge, had burned to the ground after the furnace malfunctioned. The news devastated them, but the bitter loss of their home and all their possessions was radically tempered by what the two women witnessed in Europe. They encountered the ruins of great cities, destroyed by the relentless bombing of Germany's air force. Their loss seemed minor compared to the suffering of millions in the warring European nations.

Keller lost one precious object in the fire that was truly irreplaceable: her manuscript of Sullivan's biography, representing six years of work. Determined to tell the life story of her beloved Teacher, Keller started out on the grueling task of rewriting the entire book. It would be another nine years before the book, *Teacher: Anne Sullivan Macy,* was finally published.

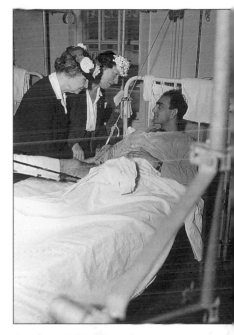

In a hospital in Georgia, Keller and Thomson visit a soldier who was wounded in France during World War II. Keller traveled to numerous military hospitals to offer encouragement to soldiers who had been blinded or deafened in battle.

In 1949, Keller works on a braillewriter, typing her manuscript for her biography of Anne Sullivan Macy. Keller had to rewrite the entire book after her original manuscript about Teacher was burned in a fire that destroyed Keller's home in 1946.

Ten months after the fire, Keller and Thomson moved into Arcan Ridge II, a new 12-room house built on the site of their former home. The rose-covered clapboard house was built almost exactly like the original to make the adjustment easier for Keller. The Library of Congress replaced 144 braille editions of Keller's library that had been destroyed by the fire, and other donations of braille books poured in from around the world.

The yard displayed a gift from the people of Japan, an illuminated, stone Japanese lantern standing 8 feet high. Its light was never to be extinguished as long as Helen lived. On the path between the garden and woods, Keller strolled with her dogs. Over the years, she had a succession of canine companions—mastiffs, bull terriers, and a springer spaniel. When evening arrived, Keller and Thomson set aside their appointments and writing projects, and enjoyed playing chess, checkers, and dominoes with specially designed boards and game pieces, and card games with cards using braille symbols.

In 1950, a high school student asked the 70-year-old Keller how she regarded old age. Keller remarked that it was a wonderful question and responded, "All my life I have tried to avoid ruts, such as doing things my ancestors did before me, or leaning on the crutches of other people's opinion, or losing my childhood sense of wonderment. I am glad to say I still have a vivid sense of wonderment. I am glad to say I still have a vivid curiosity about the world I live in. . . . It is as natural for me to believe that the richest harvest of happiness comes with age as to believe that true sight and hearing are within, not without."

These were busy years for Keller. With Thomson at her side, the two women continued to promote programs for

Keller is seen here taking a walk around Arcan Ridge. Keller and Thomson had a new 12-room house built on the site of their former home in Westport and called it Arcan Ridge II.

the physically challenged around the globe. Between 1946 and 1957, they visited schools and hospitals in 35 countries on 5 continents. For her efforts, Keller received numerous awards, including Japan's Sacred Treasure Award, Brazil's Southern Cross, the Philippines's Golden Heart, and France's Legion of Honor.

In 1957, Polly Thomson suffered a stroke and was never able to care for Keller again. Thomson died in 1960, and her ashes were interred next to Anne Sullivan Macy's at the National Cathedral in Washington, D.C.

Once again, Keller was alone, but with the help of a secretary, Evelyn Seide, and a nurse, Winifred Corbally, Keller resumed her life at Arcan Ridge. In October 1959, *The Miracle Worker,* a play about the lives of Sullivan and Keller, opened on Broadway in New York City to rave reviews. Playwright William Gibson based the script on Sullivan's letters contained in Keller's first autobiography, *The Story of My Life.* Actress Anne Bancroft played the part of Teacher and the child actress Patty Duke starred as Helen. The play was made into a highly acclaimed movie in 1962, and Bancroft and Duke repeated their stage roles, winning Oscars for their portrayals.

Keller is seen here during her 1951 trip to Africa for the American Foundation for Overseas Blind. About her enduring sense of wonderment, Keller, who was in her seventies, replied "I am glad to say I still have a vivid curiosity about the world I live in . . . the richest harvest of happiness comes with age."

On June 21, 1955, Keller studies the features of columnist Phyllis Battelle, who is at Keller's home to interview her. Keller and Thomson had recently returned from a five-month tour in the Far East, where they lectured on behalf of the blind.

In 1961, a stroke forced Keller to retire from public life; nevertheless she continued to receive many honors. In 1964, she was awarded the nation's highest civilian award, the Presidential Medal of Freedom. She was given honorary degrees from Harvard as well as from universities in India, Scotland, Germany, and South Africa.

On June 1, 1968, Helen Adams Keller died, just a few weeks before her 88th birthday. Her ashes were interred with Sullivan's and Thomson's at the National Cathedral. During the service at the National Cathedral, Senator Lister Hill of Alabama, who had been her half brother's classmate, read the following excerpt from *Journal* in a tribute to Keller: "What is so sweet as to awake from a troubled dream and behold a beloved face smiling upon you? I have to believe that such shall be our awakening from earth to heaven. My faith never wavers that each dear friend I have 'lost' is a new link between this world and the happier land beyond the morn."

Helen Keller's life is unique in the history of the world. Her story would not be so rare were it not for the intervention of another remarkable woman, Anne Sullivan

On June 24, 1965, just three days before her 85th birthday, Keller sits in her upstairs study at Arcan Ridge II. Although her traveling days were over, Keller still won accolades for her work to help the physically challenged. In 1964, President Lyndon B. Johnson awarded her the nation's highest civilian honor, the Presidential Medal of Freedom.

Macy, who, by sacrificing her own life, gave voice to her young student's remarkable mind, making it possible for Helen Keller to share her message with the world. Her message is indeed timeless; it is one of hope in the face of life's darkest adversities. It is understanding the goodness in humanity that enables people to reach out and lift up their fellow human being. And, finally, the message of Helen Keller challenges everyone to define themselves by their dreams and accomplishments rather than by their limitations.

FURTHER READING

Brooks, Van Wyck. *Helen Keller: Sketch for a Portrait.* New York: E. P. Dutton, 1956.

Harrity, Richard, and Ralph G. Martin. *The Three Lives of Helen Keller.* New York: Doubleday, 1962.

Keller, Helen. *Journal.* New York: Doubleday, Doran, 1938.

———. *Midstream: My Later Life.* New York: Doubleday, Doran, 1929.

——— . *My Religion.* New York: Doubleday, Doran, 1927.

———. *Out of the Dark.* New York: Doubleday, Page, 1913.

———. *The Story of My Life.* New York: Doubleday, Page, 1903.

———. *Teacher: Anne Sullivan Macy.* New York: Doubleday, 1955.

———. *The World I Live In.* New York: Century, 1908.

Lash, Joseph P. *Helen and Teacher: The Story of Helen Keller and Anne Sullivan Macy.* New York: Delacorte, 1980.

Ross, Ishbel. *Journey into Light.* New York: Appleton-Century Crofts, 1951.

Wepman, Dennis. *Helen Keller.* New York: Chelsea House Publishers, 1987.

White, Helen Elmira. *Valiant Companions: Helen Keller and Anne Sullivan Macy.* Philadelphia: Macrae Smith, 1959.

CHRONOLOGY

1880   Helen Adams Keller is born in Tuscumbia, Alabama, on June 27

1882   Helen loses her sight and hearing in February after an illness

1887   In March, Anne Sullivan is hired to teach Helen; on April 5, Helen first comprehends the concept of language as a means of communication, and later that month Sullivan teaches her the manual alphabet; Helen begins to learn braille in July

1888   Keller visits Perkins Institution for the Blind in Boston, Massachusetts, with Sullivan in July

1894   She begins to study at Wright-Humason School in New York City

1896   Helen's father, Arthur Keller, dies; she enters the Cambridge School for Young Ladies

1900   Keller enrolls at Radcliffe College

1903   She publishes *The Story of My Life*

1904   Keller graduates from Radcliffe

1905   Sullivan marries John Macy

1908   Keller publishes *The World I Live In*

1913   Her book, *Out of the Dark,* is published; she embarks on a lecture tour with Sullivan

1914   Anne Sullivan and John Macy separate; Polly Thomson is hired

1918–19   Keller stars in the film *Deliverance*

1919–24   Keller appears on the vaudeville circuit with Sullivan

1921   Kate Adams Keller, Helen's mother, dies

1924   Keller begins work for the American Foundation for the Blind

1927   She publishes *My Religion*

1929   Her autobiographical work *Midstream* is published

1936   Anne Sullivan Macy dies on October 20

1937   Keller tours Japan with Thomson

1938   She publishes *Journal*

1943–46	Keller visits soldiers, wounded in World War II, in military hospitals
1946–57	Keller tours 25 countries on behalf of the physically challenged
1955	She publishes *Teacher: Anne Sullivan Macy*
1960	Polly Thomson dies
1961	Keller suffers a stroke; she retires from public life
1968	Helen Adams Keller dies in Westport, Connecticut, on June 1

INDEX

PICTURE CREDITS

American Foundation for the Blind: pp. 24, 25, 39, 56, 70, 82; AP/Wide World Photos: pp. 2, 20, 30, 42, 94, 97, 99, 100, 103, 104, 106; Library of Congress: pp. 12, 26, 32, 37, 44, 49, 51, 54, 59, 60, 62, 63, 65, 67, 68, 71, 72, 73, 74, 75, 77, 80, 88; Perkins School for the Blind: pp. 22, 27, 46, 50; Smithsonian Institution: p. 16; UPI/Bettmann: pp. 52, 64, 84, 86, 89, 91, 101, 102, 105.

Lois P. Nicholson was born in Sudlersville, Maryland, and holds a bachelor of science degree in elementary education and a master's degree in education from the Salisbury State University. She is a school librarian media specialist at Cape St. Claire Elementary School near Annapolis, Maryland. She has written other biographies for Chelsea House, including *George Washington Carver, Oprah Winfrey, Michael Jackson, Casey Stengel, Nolan Ryan,* and *Lucille Ball.* In addition, she has written *Cal Ripken, Jr.: Quiet Hero* (Tidewater), *Babe Ruth: Sultan of Swat* (Goodwood Press), and *Georgia O'Keeffe* (Lucent). Ms. Nicholson also visits schools to speak to students and faculties about writing nonfiction. She lives in Baltimore, Maryland.

Jerry Lewis is the National Chairman of the Muscular Dystrophy Association (MDA) and host of the MDA Labor Day Telethon. An internationally acclaimed comedian, Lewis began his entertainment career in New York and then performed in a comedy team with singer and actor Dean Martin from 1946 to 1956. Lewis has appeared in many films— including *The Delicate Delinquent, Rock a Bye Baby, The Bellboy, Cinderfella, The Nutty Professor, The Disorderly Orderly,* and *The King of Comedy*—and his comedy perfor- mances continue to delight audiences around the world.

John Callahan is a nationally syndicated cartoonist and the author of an illustrated autobiography, *Don't Worry, He Won't Get Far on Foot.* He has also produced three cartoon collections: *Do Not Disturb Any Further, Digesting the Child Within,* and *Do What He Says! He's Crazy!!!* He has recently been the subject of feature articles in the *New York Times Magazine,* the *Los Angeles Times Magazine,* and the *Cleveland Plain Dealer,* and has been profiled on "60 Minutes." Callahan resides in Portland, Oregon.